A SPIRITUALITY
FOR THE
TWENTY-FIRST
CENTURY

A SPIRITUALITY
FOR THE
TWENTY-FIRST
CENTURY

—— AIDAN NICHOLS, O.P. ——

Our Sunday Visitor Publishing Division
Our Sunday Visitor, Inc.
Huntington, Indiana 46750

Our Sunday Visitor Publishing Division
Our Sunday Visitor, Inc.
200 Noll Plaza
Huntington, IN 46750

ISBN: 1-931709-54-8 (Inventory No. T31)
LCCN: 2002112337

Cover design by Monica Haneline
Cover photo copyright © 2002 Comstock, Inc.
Interior design by Sherri L. Hoffman
Interior art by Andy Kurzen

PRINTED IN THE UNITED STATES OF AMERICA

CONTENTS

Acknowledgments   7

I. The Master Class   9

II. Eight Masters   15

    1. Flower Among Thorns: Thérèse of Lisieux and
       the Love of Simplicity   17

    2. Worshiping Spirit: Columba Marmion and
       the Love of the Liturgy   35

    3. Great Heart: Gilbert Keith Chesterton and
       the Love of the Virtues   49

    4. Poet of Faith: Charles Péguy and the Love of Hope   65

    5. Martyr of Israel: Edith Stein and the Love of Wisdom 81

    6. Passionate Sage: Charles Williams and the Love
       of the Human City   95

    7. Theological Artist: Leonid Ouspensky and the
       Love of Sacred Beauty   113

    8. Looking to the Other: Jules Monchanin and
       the Love of the Trinity   131

III. A Spirituality for the Twenty-first Century   145

Notes   151

Bibliography   163

ACKNOWLEDGMENTS

This book owes its existence to the initiative of Michael Dubruiel of Our Sunday Visitor, who, I hope, will not now regret his confidence in the author. Parts of Chapters Two, Three, and Four have appeared elsewhere, and I thank the relevant publishers — the Saint Austin Press (London) and Family Publications (Oxford) — for their kindness in permitting reprinting of these sections.

All of the figures whose inspirational force I have tried to capture in these pages — whether they be saints or sinners — are beloved in my eyes. I hope something of what I have seen in them is communicated here to others.

AIDAN NICHOLS, O.P.
Blackfriars
Cambridge
Old St. Gregory's Day, 2002

I. THE MASTER CLASS

There is only one Master, the Christ. And yet the same Lord who declared that the disciple is not above his Master also predicted that his disciples would do greater works than his own — which a sound theology might explain as their manifesting of his grace in more varied and comprehensive settings than the Tree of Calvary and the Empty Tomb from where all spiritual health, of whatever kind, ultimately flows.

Introduction

I do not propose to do much by way of defining "spirituality." In the context of orthodox Catholicism, its meaning is sufficiently clear. It means so to live the faith that one grows in love of God and one's neighbor. The eight figures described in this book have been chosen because the author considers they can help the well-disposed reader to do exactly that.

Looking back at the twentieth century, one can now see that it was one of history's grimmest. The essays in this book touch on two of its most horrendous episodes: the carnage of the trench fighting in the First World War of 1914-1918 and the Holocaust of European Jewry from 1942 to 1945. As if by compensation, in the same century there have been raised up a goodly number of masterful witnesses to Christian spirituality, the Christian life.

The Idea of a 'Master Class'

I take the idea of a "master class" from either music or painting. In the first instance, it can be seen as a class where a supreme crafts-man presides for the benefit of pupils. In one sense, none of the figures whom I display in this short study would, I am sure, wish to be so elevated above the rest of the Church. There is only one Master, the Christ. And yet the same Lord who declared that the disciple is not above his Master also predicted that his disciples would do greater works than his own — which a sound theology might explain as their manifesting of his grace in more varied and comprehensive settings than the Tree of Calvary and the Empty

Tomb from where all spiritual health, of whatever kind, ultimately flows. And in that sense, the "class" Christ holds as the prime and principal Prophet (thus St. Thomas Aquinas hails him) is intended to form future masters, who in their turn can go on to teach others, by word and example, how to live, suffer, and triumph in the life of grace. That is how I mean to use the phrase "master class" in relation to the people who are the subject of this book.

The reader will find here women and men, monks and worldlings, writers and painters, stay-at-homes and travelers to exotic parts. There should be, then, something for everyone. But more than this, I hope that everyone will find something in all of them.

A Stroll Through the Woods

Permit me now a change of metaphor. It is part of the meaning of being "catholic" — universal — that the Holy Spirit does not cut the materials to make our spiritual models from the wood of one tree (unless it be that Tree of the Cross). Here in these pages are applewood and acacia, hornbeam and sequoia. May we rejoice in the great forest of the *Catholica* and take our bearings from its many glades.

Of the figures I describe, two lived and died outside the visible unity of the Church. Trees can seed themselves across waterways, waterways that may define the boundaries of a wood. Cannot bridges be built to enable wanderers to enjoy their shade? It is in that spirit that an Anglican writer and an Orthodox writer and painter appear in these pages.

The conclusion to this book will argue that our walk has been no random meander. The path we shall follow will be like those laid own in the classical gardens of Japan. Influenced by Zen Buddhism, those paths form, typically, a circuit with a mystical meaning. Here, too, there is a planned, comprehensive intent.

A Program for the Future

Allow me to revert, then, to my original concept. The eight figures selected in this "master class" were not chosen by accident. Rather, the themes they privilege in their teaching constitute in their totality the main features that a Catholic spirituality for the future needs to exhibit, the principal aspirations it needs to encourage and to shape.

II. EIGHT MASTERS

Thérèse of Lisieux
Columba Marmion
Gilbert Keith Chesterton
Charles Péguy
Edith Stein
Charles Williams
Leonid Ouspensky
Jules Monchanin

ONE

❧

Flower Among Thorns
Thérèse of Lisieux and the Love of Simplicity

Introduction

One of the last acts of the twentieth-century papacy was to take up the name of a middle-class girl who lived all her short life in a couple of French provincial towns and declare its bearer a doctor of the Church. On October 19, 1997, Pope John Paul II proclaimed Thérèse Martin to be such, and thus a teacher of faith and morals — Christian believing and Christian living — worthy to be mentioned in the same breath as an Augustine or a Basil.[1] Thérèse of Lisieux died just before the twentieth century opened, but her fame as a spiritual teacher reached its height just as that century expired. So she is well placed to be the first of our "master class": a maker of spirituality for the twenty-first century that is now upon us.

She was born in an elegant home in the Rue Saint-Blaise in Alençon on January 2, 1873, to comfortably well-off — and certainly very pious — parents, who owned both a lace-making business and a jeweler's-cum-watchmaker's enterprise in the town. It was after the death of her mother in August 1877 that the family — M. Martin and his five daughters — moved to Lisieux to be closer to the household of the Guérins, the deceased woman's brother and sister-in-law. (Lisieux is a once-beautiful city, owing to its many houses with sculpted wooden facades in the classical

Norman style but sadly disfigured by Allied bombing during the Second World War. It will always be inseparable from the name of Thérèse.)

Her childhood environment was pleasant enough: the Martin villa, "Les Buissonets," set in a substantial garden dotted with clumps of yucca trees; her own room, with its birdcages and clutter of devotional objects; the surrounding Norman countryside, from family ambles through which, later accompanied by her spaniel, Tom, she acquired her love of flowers. This bourgeois Catholic setting formed her early sensibility. One might be forgiven for thinking her life was hardly likely to exhibit heroic features.

She did not enjoy her schooling at the prestigious Benedictine abbey of Notre Dame du Pré, being particularly allergic to group games. However, the school chaplain, the Abbé Domin, noted her facility with the catechism (calling her, presciently as things turned out, his "little doctor"), and she managed history and geography well enough. Trips to the fashionable watering places on the Channel coast — Deauville, Trouville, and Honfleur — introduced her to a less ecclesiastical world (though an oyster shell painted by her on one of these jaunts does not depart from the preferred iconography of her paintings: the Cross and the Sacred Heart).

A problem of scrupulosity (for which she sought the intercession of her dead baby brothers and sisters) made her confessions and communions — her Eucharistic piety was already intense — somewhat purgatorial. She remained "a hypersensitive child . . . [who] would cry for nothing."[2] Only what she called her "complete conversion" at Christmas 1886 ended this emotional malaise. That conversion had nothing to do (apparently) with born-again Christianity. It seemed to consist simply in an effort of self-control by which, rather than burst into tears at the announcement that some childish family ritual was being held for the last time, she managed to behave as serenely as a queen. She considered it to be the moment when she left her natural childhood behind and became a child in a quite new sense — on which more anon.

Both of her elder sisters had entered the Carmel of Lisieux. Thérèse intended to follow them on the first anniversary of her "conversion." Two themes stand out in what is known of her attitudes at this period. She wanted to apply the blood of Jesus to sinners, especially great sinners; and she accepted the dictum of the "gentleman saint" (and, incidentally, patron of writers) Francis de Sales, "A sad saint is a sorry saint." How these motifs could be united, the future would show.

In point of fact, the local clergy were unwilling to allow so young a girl to enter monastic life. Her participation in her father's visit to the Vatican for Leo XIII's jubilee put a certain pressure on the Lisieux authorities, though the deadly serious candidate was also capable of lighthearted enjoyment of the rail journey via Lucerne, the Alps, and a variety of Italian cities. On arrival at Rome, she expressed her opinion that the pope was so old as to be almost dead. (He was to outlive her by six years.) The lengthy excursion gave Thérèse her closest contact so far with priests. She added a new desideratum to her intercession list: the holiness of the clergy.

Back in Lisieux, her bishop (a good scholar, the editor of the works of the early Scholastic theologian Richard of St. Victor in the *Patrologia Latina*) consented to the fifteen-year-old entering the Carmel, which she did on April 9 (the transferred feast of the Annunciation), 1889.

Her Writings

So began not only her cloistered life but also the writings —
jottings, mainly, though the principal autobiographical memoir
was written as continuous prose, without draft or corrections —
contained in notebooks costing altogether a couple of francs.

Aside from her catechism, spiritual reading, and what she
could understand of the texts of the Mass and Divine Office, she
was, of course, completely unschooled as a theologian. But theologians have done a lot to lay out her spirituality for the benefit
of the rest of the Church — a good omen, hopefully, for the
enterprise on which I am engaged in this book![3]

It is easy to come close to her. The text composed by her fellow
nuns on the basis of two substantial autobiographical fragments
(known as Manuscripts A and C) — "improved" by the blue pencil
of severe Premonstratensian canons to whom it was submitted, en-
riched by the addition of a long letter to her sister Pauline (Manuscript B), and finally published as "The Story of a Soul" — has been
known for over a century. (The *Histoire d'une Ame* first appeared in
1898.[4]) The collection of papers released by the Carmel of Lisieux in
1956 under the title "Autobiographical Manuscripts" did much to
correct faulty perceptions caused by well-meaning overediting.[5] And
a real sense of immediate *rapport* was created by the publication in
1961 of the forty-seven authentic photographs taken (mostly) by
her sister Céline and edited by the Discalced Carmelite Père François
de Sainte-Marie.[6] In 1971, the centenary edition of her "works" began with what is in many ways the most revealing collection of her
sayings, much of it taken from the witnesses who contributed to the
beatification and canonization inquiries: the "Last Conversations of
St. Thérèse of the Child Jesus."[7] However, it is not from any of these
excellent works that I propose to begin but from a very different
source that will act as a foil to show off her star.

Nietzsche and Thérèse

On November 20, 1888, Friedrich Nietzsche wrote a letter to a Danish historian of literature, Georg Brandes, in which he announced his forthcoming book, *Ecce Homo*. Man, that work will argue, is great by virtue of his capacity for sacrifice — understood as a struggle to overcome the limits of his finitude, to take the place once occupied by God. Nietzsche sensed the exactness with which this scheme contradicts that of the Gospel:

> The name of the book is *Ecce Homo*, and it represents a sort of assassination, without any mercy, for the Crucified One; it ends with thunder and lightning against anything which is Christian or in any way contaminated by Christianity. . . . The whole thing is a prelude to "The Revaluation of All Value," a work which I have already finished. I tell you that within two years I'll have the whole earth in convulsions.

About the same day on which Nietzsche wrote these words, an obscure member of the French provincial middle class received a letter, dated November 18, from her niece Thérèse Martin, then a postulant, aged fifteen, in the Carmel at Lisieux:

> This morning, at Communion I prayed hard to Jesus to fill you to the full with his joys. . . . Alas, joys are not what he has been sending us for some time; it is the Cross and only the Cross that he gives us to rest upon. . . . Oh, my dearest aunt, if it were only I that must suffer, I would not mind, but I know the great part you take in our trial. I should like to take every sorrow from you for your feast, to take all your burdens to myself.

The contrast in the message of these letters can hardly fail to strike us. It certainly struck the first heavyweight philosopher-theologian to write about Thérèse — the German Jesuit Erich Przywara. In his studies *Heroisch* and *Humanitas*, he advances his own thought precisely by contrasting Thérèse and Nietzsche.[8]

For Przywara, Nietzsche rightly sensed man's pull toward the Absolute but wrongly interpreted it as a call to deny human finitude. Nietzsche grasped that man must live sacrificially, ever ready for struggle, but having no conception of grace, his commendation of heroism led inevitably to brutality and despair. Thérèse, too, is ready for sacrifice; but renouncing all exterior greatness, and surmounting the temptation of revolt against God, she attains a grandeur veiled in littleness by following the route of a sober, modest abandonment of self to the love of God. Przywara speaks of Nietzsche and Thérèse standing "eyeball to eyeball," making much of the coincidence of the year 1888 to which the two letters cited belong: the year when one entered a lunatic asylum, the other the desert of Carmel. She is the perfect antidote to falsified heroism.

It may be a little unfair to quote Nietzsche in this fashion. His letter was written shortly before the outbreak of his mental illness: hence the extravagance of the language. Moreover, it reveals only one side of a complex man who let his complexity get the better of him and finally broke under its weight. But that very concession sharpens the contrast with Thérèse. With her, one is always in context. She once mentioned that she began to accept the love of Christ and his Cross when she was three. She died at the age of twenty-four, in incredible suffering, with the words, "My God, I love you." This single-mindedness, this consistency of central purpose from beginning to end, becomes the more startling the better acquainted one is with Thérèse of Lisieux.

We must not be deceived by the style of expression of her letters, or indeed her poems, the memoir she left (under obedience), and her other manuscripts. The poetic taste of the middle class of the French provinces; the imagery of flowers, perfumes, and toys; the fondness for such adjectives as "little" and "sweet" — all of this emphasizes her lack of surface originality. Such cloying verbal imagery is mirrored in the sentimental iconography she favored in visual art, though there probably was little choice in the matter, as taste in sacred art in the period was generally dictated by a combination of debased Romanticism and mass production. (This is a pity, because she had a real talent for drawing and painting.) What a contrast to the crisp poetic images and austere artwork fashioned by her fellow-Carmelite John of the Cross! That such a searing flame as hers should have been hidden under a camouflage of *fin-de-siècle* ornament is a challenge to us. It is not *chic*, not cool. It is a trial to our intellectual pride.

Anonymity and the 'Little Way'

When she was on her sickbed in the convent she had belonged to ever since she left school in the same Norman town, she overheard a conversation between the novices beneath an open window. After the death of a nun, the superior commonly sends a death notice with a biographical note to other communities. What she overheard was the novices remarking how difficult it would be for the prioress to think up anything to say when Sister Thérèse died. The object of these comments rejoiced at them. Anonymity would be one of the features of the "Little Way" she both lived and taught. Neither ecstasies nor special penances are necessary for holiness. Indeed, far from striking such dramatic poses, one should seek to be quite unnoticed — and in the practice of virtue, not let the left hand know what the right hand is doing.

No matter how apparently insignificant our lives on the plane of tangible effect on society, people, or affairs, those same lives are shot through with significance just because they are *ours*. They cannot be too "little" for this to be the case. Zero, she pointed out, by itself has no value. But once placed alongside *one*, it suddenly acquires extraordinary potency — always provided it is put on the proper side, which is after, not before! She enjoyed an extremely vivid awareness of the infinite value of each single person, once he or she is seen in relation to God.

Her attitude to anonymity seems to have undergone a change, however, in the course of 1895, when she began signing her letters "the very *little* Thérèse.' The eminent Theresian scholar Pierre Descouvemont explains:

> Until then Therese had used the vocabulary of littleness to express her desire to remain hidden from the eyes of the world and her determination not to seek the love and recognition of her sisters. Henceforth, she would use it to express her joyful hope that the more she felt her littleness before God, the more she would enter into his intimate fellowship.[9]

Of course, this was not sheerly self-regarding. It was a doctrine, a vision, of God's relation with any and every recipient of his kindness. Thus, speaking of the grace of God at work in her sister Céline, Thérèse remarked that he was prouder of what he had done in her soul, in its littleness and poverty, than of having created millions of suns and the whole expanse of the heavens. Sayings like these tend to produce something of an optional illusion. The "sweet," "petite" girl disappears and before one stands an immense, awe-inspiring, timeless figure, companion of the prophets and apostles, fathers and mystics of the Church.

Or is it an illusion? Her sister said of her that she revealed her strength "in a multitude of slight, almost microscopic acts." There were, for example, the acts needed if charity were to reign in relations with a touchy and unpredictable superior; or a depressive nun subject to alarming mood swings; or a sister who considered that bourgeois girls who knew how to tend roses but not plant potatoes had no place in the Carmel. Or, perhaps worst of all, the rather rigid nun (a "potted lily," Thérèse called her) who had the uncanny knack of irritating Thérèse by almost everything she did and who believed till long after Thérèse's death that she was one of her favorite sisters.

Then we must keep in mind the misinterpretations and rebuffs she experienced; the frequent coldness, both physical and emotional, of the human environment; the torture of doubt about the reality of a future life (particularly in Paschaltide 1896, the penultimate Easter of her life); the physical agony as her illness took final hold (suffocation, insomnia, bedsores, constipation, and gangrene of the intestines: "I would never have believed it possible to suffer so much! Never! Never!"). This was the raw material from which she made her "little, nameless, unremembered acts of kindness and love," and became the woman of whom it was said when she could not appear for recreation, "There will be no laughter today. Sister Thérèse is not here."

Carmelite spirituality was — and is — frequently regarded as daunting. It seems to be for ascetic athletes, or for those who combine high mystical graces with an almost Teutonic emphasis on their systematic schematization. This appears especially true of Sanjuanist spirituality, the thinking of St. John of the Cross. But this was not how Thérèse saw St John.[10] She took from him something far simpler. In the *Maxims and Spiritual Counsels*, John remarks that at the eventide of our days we shall be judged on love. In his writings, Thérèse found reflected the fundamental insight of her Little Way. To offer oneself to merciful love, it is not necessary to be a perfect victim. It is enough to offer oneself as one is — though not to canonize mediocrity, which is how *we* are likely to take such a thought! Rather, it is because the depths of our poverty call forth the depths of God's mercy. When we cease to rely on our own weakness, we can succeed in relying on his strength.

Spiritual Childhood

However, her way was not "little" simply because it used the most humdrum events — we might almost say the non-events — of daily existence. It was little because it involved recovering the posture of a child. It was the Little Way of *spiritual childhood*. (The term was first used by her sister Pauline — her second prioress, Mother Agnes — in 1907, but it precisely expresses Thérèse's meaning.)

People were and are suspicious of this notion, especially in a cloistered nun barely out of adolescence. Has not modern psychology done away with the picture of the loving, good, and humble child? The ambivalence of our feeling-life develops early. Children are at times little monsters of egoism. But all of us have gone through a phase of (morally neutral) utter dependence when there was no alternative to trusting our mother. We could not foresee hazards and had to leave them to her foresight. We simply *had* to trust. Now this is interesting, because the archetypal child we once were (in that kind of way) is still alive in every one of us. To regress to it on the natural level would be a serious form of neurosis. To find our way back to it on the supernatural level is the highest form of maturity.

"As one whom his mother comforts, so I will comfort you" are words of the Lord to Israel through the prophet Isaiah (66:13).

For this to be possible, there must be a child on the receiving end. When Christ taught his disciples to pray, he brought them into the heart of his own Child-Father relationship. His initiation of them presupposes the basic condition he lays down for discipleship — namely, that of becoming like a little child. His own earthly relation with the Father will come to its climax in the Passion, which, in St. Luke's account, closes with his using the Jewish child's "good night" prayer: "Father, into thy hands I commit my spirit" (23:46). To find the Father specifically as Father, the disciple has no option but to become a child.

The first step here is leaving natural childhood behind. The security — happy and healthy though it be — of parental dependence is too finite and transitory to be the sort proper to a spirit open to the infinite. The personality must develop; the thrust toward emancipation is legitimate and necessary. It is a precondition for the discovery of the infinite-within-the-finite in the values of childhood.

As a child, Thérèse was dreadfully overprotected, and there was a real danger that she would remain all her life childishly dependent on a domineering elder sister (Pauline, her "second mother") and an indulgent father. If this had happened, she would never have discovered the way of spiritual childhood, because it is a way characterized by total independence of everything and everyone except God. But on Christmas night 1886, in another "overhearing" scene — where, this time, she heard her father expressing relief that this would be the last year he was going to put "surprise" gifts in her slippers — she received, as she later put it, "the grace to leave my childhood days behind.'[11]

When, three years after this episode she entered the Carmel — a world of regular observance, mortification, the hard discipline of obedience, and the harder discipline of living daily with a small group in a confined space with no future reprieve — she entered an enclosure with no escape hatch, save upward. Perforce she looked upward (it was why she had entered, to pray!). But in a Carmelite tradition much influenced by the reparatory, expiatory spirituality — stemming from the seventeenth-century formation of the French Carmels and intensified by response to the "Godless" revolutions of 1789 and 1870, she found at first only a God of fear and majesty. This was a God who could be reached only by a great ladder whose lowest rung was outside her reach. Or at best, a God of two faces: one loving, and the other severe, unsearchable.

Under the pressure of this experience, she discovered in the Scriptures — notably, in the Gospels — "a quite new little way," which simply consisted in seeing God as a loving Father and herself as a little child. She rediscovered, that is, her own childhood — its serene, loving trustfulness, and its affection and openness — but now unlimited by her family, uncircumscribed by any finite context of support. (It was just as well, for to her other crosses would soon be added the intermittent madness — now thought to be arteriosclerosis — of her beloved natural father, Louis Martin.)

This was a childhood thrown open to the God of creation and redemption, to the Father who, through his Son, Jesus Christ, asks from his children a love as wide as the world.

Here she was assisted by the historic Carmelite devotion to the childhood of Christ. In 1628, a Bohemian noblewoman, Polyxena de Pernshtejir, had entrusted a waxen statue of the Infant Jesus to the Carmelites of Prague; about the same time, at the Carmel of Beaune, one of the sisters, Marguerite of the Blessed Sacrament (Marguerite Parigot) experienced visions of the Child Jesus as King of kings and Lord of lords. It all picked up an emphasis on the Incarnation going right back to the "Spanish mothers," the beginnings of the Carmelite reform, in Ávila.

Characteristically, however, Thérèse changed this formula to the "Divine Little Beggar of Christmas." In Jesus, the Almighty One asks only our simple love.

Again, she had long revered the Holy Face of Christ, which seemed to demand reparation for "outrages" committed against it through blasphemy, indifference, or the "apostasy" of France. That had been the point of the "Atoning Confraternity of the Holy Face," into which, along with her father and sisters, she had been enrolled in 1885. A nun of the Carmel of Tours who had died in the "Year of Revolutions," 1848, had done much to spread this spirituality of reparation for outrage. But what now predominated with Thérèse was the contemplation of that face as, quite simply, the Face of Love.

And this enabled her to see the intimate unity binding together the two "titles" that, along with other Carmelites, she placed after her name. (Strictly speaking, they were known as "titles of devotion." Thérèse of the Child Jesus and the Holy Face called hers "all her claim to nobility, all her riches, all her hope."[12]) The Child and the face of the suffering Adult Christ communicated a single message, because, from the first moment of his consciousness, Jesus had offered himself to the Father in an outpouring of love of which his Passion was the only possible outcome. Hence, the coat of arms she devised for the end of her first manuscript in 1896: the Child Jesus dreams of his future Holy Face— that is, his suffering and death.

Entry Into Trinitarian Life: Love Alone

The Irish Carmelite theologian Noel Dermot O'Donoghue wrote:

> Essentially Thérèse's way of childhood is a way of entry into the Trinitarian mystery of Fatherhood, Sonship and that

eternal breathing of love which is the Holy Spirit. The life
and death of Jesus, in its total trust, is the revelation of
eternal childhood in history. This childhood is not easy to
achieve because it demands detachment from the posses-
sive self and from all that is finite and particular. This is the
negative side: positively, it is a deep warmth and tender-
ness, an all-fathering, all-mothering love, for the child shares
now in God's attitude to creation. Mystical prayer is essentially the expression of a love that has grown beyond the
particular, especially of particular persons. This love is full
of pathos and loneliness, for it is an exile in the world. It is
always being misunderstood in its most innocent and spon-
taneous manifestations, for the world can only understand
love grossly, having lost childhood. It is deeply marked with
the sign of the Cross, otherwise it is not genuine. Yet if
there is any state that may be termed blessed and heavenly
it is here that it is found.[13]

In June 1895, while making the Way of the Cross privately
in choir, Thérèse was suddenly seized with so violent an expression of the love of God that she at first believed herself to be
immersed in fire. (She had almost gone up in literal flames the
previous January when acting the part of Joan of Arc in a play
put on for recreation, thanks to the carelessness of the sister re-
sponsible for staging the execution scene.) In a statement omit-
ted from the autobiography, she describes herself as burning with
love for God. She took this as a sign that she was to make an
offering of herself as "holocaust victim" — not to the divine justice (that had been the terrible way of some of her predecessors),
but to the merciful love of God. Love must be repaid by love.
The first pulmonary hemorrhage, revealing the extent to which

an unsuspected tuberculosis had already ravaged her body, took place the following Good Friday. Toward the end she wrote:

> Now I have no wishes left except the wish to love Our Lord to distraction. Those childish desires of mine seem to have vanished. What is there left for me to desire? . . . Only love really attracts me. . . . Now resignation is my only guide, the only compass I have to steer by.[14]

She had discovered the theological truth that, in her own words:

> If the Church was a body composed of different members, it couldn't lack the noblest of all, it must have a heart, and a heart burning with love. And I realized that this love was the true motive force which enabled the other members of the Church to act; if it ceased to function the Apostles would forget to teach the gospel, the Martyrs would refuse to shed their blood. Love, in fact, is the vocation which includes all others; it's a universe of its own, comprising all time and space — it's eternal. Beside myself with joy I cried out, Jesus, my Love: I've found my vocation and my vocation is love.[15]

She knew that this vocation would last forever, promising, "I will come back again, I will shower down roses on this earth."[16]

Her death occurred in complete obscurity on September 30, 1897. Two days later, the novelist Leo Tolstoy, on his Russian estate in faraway Yasnaya Poliana, made an entry in his diary:

> I imagined vividly what a joyful, peaceful, and completely free life this would be: to be able to dedicate oneself entirely to God, that is, if one intended in all situations which life

presents only to accept his will — during illness, when one has been insulted, in humiliation, in suffering, in all temptations, and in death. In that case, death would be nothing but the taking on of a new task.

That flawed genius was struggling for a goal to which he had come closer than many. He beheld it, yet was far removed from it. And Sister Thérèse had reached it. One begins to understand the words of the social philosopher Emmanuel Mounier, "Thérèse is a ruse of the Holy Spirit."[17] She had given Mother Agnes some final directives about the publication of her manuscripts. Thérèse now welcomed it: "People will be more aware of the gentleness of God."[18]

TWO

❧❧

Worshiping Spirit
Columba Marmion and the Love of the Liturgy

Introduction

Joseph Marmion was Thérèse Martin's senior by fifteen years.[19] He was Dublin-born, the son of a prosperous mid-Victorian Irish corn merchant and a French mother. He grew up a merry lad with a reflective mind. When, after many moons had passed, he became abbot of the Walloon monastery of Maredsous, the combination of his great girth, his whimsy, and the remarkable clarity of his theological exposition inevitably suggested a monastic G. K. Chesterton — though the humor did not find its way into the texts he left behind.

In 1874, when only sixteen, Marmion entered the archdiocesan seminary of the Holy Cross, Clonliffe, in the Dublin suburb of Drumcondra. There he would enjoy the first of a series of intuitive experiences, or "lights" as he called them — a momentary glimpse of the divine infinity. A stranger to all the "extraordinary" and, *a fortiori*, the paranormal features of mysticism, his mind was none the less sharpened and deepened by graced insights into the historic revelation and its bearing on Christian life.

This added savor to understanding, and power to preaching and lecturing for the grown man, but he did not regard it as a substitute for study. Indeed, his aptitude for both philosophy and theology led his superiors to send him from Clonliffe to the

Roman college of Propaganda Fidei, where he heard and was influenced by Francesco Satolli, later cardinal and a prime mover in that revival of the thought of St. Thomas Aquinas that was so marked a feature of the pontificate of Leo XIII. Satolli gave the young Marmion a solid formation in Thomism, which would remain, along with Scripture (notably the Pauline letters) and the Fathers, the source of his spiritual teaching.

The Monk

Though Marmion, like many of those who are birds of passage in Rome, treated a visit to the tomb of St. Benedict on Monte Cassino as *de rigueur*, his option for the Benedictine life, at a time when no monastery of that religious family existed in Ireland,[20] was fortuitous. (In a Christian perspective, we should say, rather, "providential.") Shortly after his priestly ordination on the feast of Corpus Christi 1881, he had contact, via a Belgian fellow seminarian, with Dom Rudesind Salvado, a missionary abbot engaged in planting both Catholic Christianity and Spanish Benedictinism among the aboriginals of Western Australia. Marmion at once saw the congruence of such a lifeway with the origins of the Church of the Irish — with Columbanus, Brendan, and Columba, whose name he would take at his monastic clothing. A pilgrimage to Iona in 1882 would bring back some words addressed to him by the founding abbot of Maredsous, Dom Placid Wolter, when he visited his Belgian confrere at the great Neo-Gothic pile rising amid its workshops and schoolrooms near Namur: "You have much more of a vocation than your friend."[21]

In 1886, accordingly, Marmion abandoned the life of a secular clergyman at Clonliffe (he had taught philosophy, with chaplain craft to nuns and pastoral work in the Dublin prisons as important sidelines) and took the habit of the Beuron Congregation of black monks, to which, until the disturbance caused by the German occupation of Belgium, the Walloon abbey belonged.

What did he seek? He wanted, in the first place, a communal prayer life, copying into his notebook George Herbert's lines:

> Though private prayer be a brave design
> Yet public hath more promises, more love.
> And love's a weight to hearts, to eyes a sign
> We are all but cold suitors; let us move
> Where it is warmest:
> Leave thy six and seven;
> Pray with the most; for where most pray is heaven.[22]

And secondly, he sought obedience, as a means of the perfecting of Christian discipleship, of detachment, purification, and growth in the love of God. (Without these accompaniments, which guarantee evangelical seriousness, love of the Liturgy can degenerate into aestheticism or ritualism.)

While he was at one point a candidate for the projected revitalization of the monasteries of a mission country, Brazil, obedience to Rule and abbot took him on a very different journey from that *peregrinatio pro Christo* ("wandering for Christ") of the ancient Celtic monks that he originally, if romantically, envisaged.

His "career" is easily described. After a decade as a monk of Maredsous — though hardly a "simple" monk, since he taught philosophy and theology in the abbey, was a master of ceremonies, and much in demand as preacher and retreat-giver in the parishes and convents of Francophone Belgium — he became in 1899 the first prior of the new Beuronese study house at Louvain. There, at Mont César, his task was to ensure pedagogic parity between the fledgling Benedictine "hall" and the older, more assured, teaching foundations of the Jesuits and Dominicans. More reading, rigor, and system were called for in the preparing of his lectures, though he insisted that all must remain imbued with the distinctively monastic spirit of the Liturgy and *lectio divina* (meditative pondering).

Abbot Marmion

In 1909, the then abbot of Maredsous, Hildebrand de Hemptinne — who simultaneously, as first abbot-primate of the Benedictines, enjoyed the abbacy of Sant'Anselmo on the Aventine in Rome — was prevailed upon to resign the Belgian half of his double charge, and Marmion succeeded him as third shepherd of monks in that house. He could now concentrate, accordingly, on what he was best at — the role of *doctor*, of teacher of wise doctrine.

This is not to say that Marmion considered an abbot to be simply a theologian in residence. Well attested are his specifically fatherly qualities (for that is what the Greek word *abbas* signifies), and notably his frankness and simplicity in dealing with others, his evident goodness of heart, his capacity to lift the spirits of others, his considerateness in seeking their help or service, and his respect for their dignity. At the same time, he always appealed to *super*natural motives in his dealings with them: this regime was no mere humanism. These qualities of his abbatial government are reflected in the tone of his writings, not least on the Liturgy.

The last decade of his life was turbulent in a way that no reader of his conferences could guess. With the advent of the First World War in August 1914, his position in Belgium was scarcely tenable. He was, after all, a subject of the united crowns of England and Ireland. As German troops advanced into Flanders, he fled through Holland, disguised as (of all things) a cattle dealer. Embarking on a ship, he made straight for safe harbor with the monks of Caldey, who were erstwhile Anglican Religious, living on an island off the Welsh coast, whom he had helped to reconcile with the Catholic Church. Twenty-three student-monks of Maredsous followed in three waves, and were dispersed to both Caldey and Benedictine houses in England, until such time as Marmion could acquire a "scratch" studium for them in County Wexford.

An abbot *in absentia* is, however, an unlovely thing, and he was forced to retrace his steps to Maredsous, where he would diplomatically absent himself from the official visits of the kaiser and the governor-general in the remaining years of the war. His own last years — he died, prematurely worn out by the amplitude of his undertaking and his physique, in 1923 — were complicated and saddened by not always well-judged attempts to disengage Benedictinism from the German predominance that the excellencies of the Beuron Congregation had won during the pontificates of Leo XIII, Pius X, and Benedict XV.

The Theologian

His reputation will, in any case, always rest chiefly on the spiritual theology outlined in his great trilogy: *Christ the Life of the Soul*, *Christ in His Mysteries*, and *Christ the Ideal of the Monk* — the latter not so *recherché* as might be thought, since for Marmion monastic spirituality is above all the spirituality of the early Christian springtime, but in *full vigor*.[23] These works are all-important, though the remaining eight books, letters, and some articles are required for an all-round view of his message. We must examine his overall "Gospel": it is the context of his teaching on liturgical prayer.

Christ the Life of the Soul is undoubtedly the fundamental text for Marmion's thought. It is unapologetically God-centered. Only God, author of our salvation, can make known to us what he desires of us if we are to attain to him. Tragically, people fritter away energy through misconceptions of holiness, or by losing themselves in minutiae of religious observance, when what is needed is the fullest possible synthetic view, the amplest panorama, of the divine plan. Such is the fruitfulness of the divine thought that it can fail to mature only through our fault — not by virtue of any insufficiency of its own. That metaphor of fruitfulness, with its resonance of the richness of God's self-offer, recurs time and again in Marmion, a presage of its role in an equally Trinitarian Catholic thinker later in the century, Hans Urs von Balthasar.

What, then, *is* the divine plan? From first to last, it is a *Trinitarian* mystery. The fullness and fruitfulness of the exchange of the divine Persons are the source of their bliss. God, who is always Father, since he is never without the Son, wills to extend that Fatherhood, not to add to his own plenitude but for the enrichment of others. Through the Incarnation, the only Son epiphanizes in the creation so as to become the First-born of all who, first redeemed by him, will go on to receive him. And this allows Marmion to devise that definition of holiness that gives his book its title:

> Holiness . . . is a mystery of divine life communicated and received: communicated in God, from the Father to the Son by an ineffable generation; communicated by the Son to the humanity which he personally unites to himself in the Incarnation; then restored to souls by this humanity and received by each of them in the measure of their special predestination . . . [cf. Eph 4:7], so that Christ is truly *the life of the soul* because he is the source and giver of life.[24]

Until the Parousia, this self-communication of God will constantly eventuate in the Church, not just for our salvation but also for God's glory, since the latter consists in the manifesting of the divine perfections through the gifts God bestows on creatures.

That is supremely true of our raising up through the Incarnation and Atonement, with their consummation in the Resurrection and Ascension, so as to share with Christ the divine life. In the language of Christian Scholasticism, fused as that is with the idiom of Bible and Liturgy in Marmion's work, Christ is the source of our sanctification because he is its *exemplary* cause, the model for our engraced activity; its *meritorious* cause since he deserved this grace on our behalf; and its *efficacious* cause since he produces grace in us through the contact we have with him by faith, as he once provided healing through the touching of his garment by the *Hemorrhissa*, the woman with a hemorrhage. Let us look briefly at each of these in turn.

Notice, *first*, that in his role as model, Jesus is not for Marmion chiefly a pattern for *human* virtue, a "man for others." Rather, it is in the *divine* personhood and nature, which by his enmanment he brings within our reach, that we must imitate him. In the uncreated "filiation," the essential Sonship, which his human comportment displays, he is the type of our own supernatural sonship of the Father. For the eternal being of the Son is *ad Patrem* ("toward the Father"), and his humanity consents to be carried along by this divine current. We can imitate this ourselves, thanks to the grace of divine sonship; and we do so in so far as we lay our personality before the Father and ask him to be by his Spirit — as he is for the humanity of Christ — the supreme mover in our life. This is what we study when we search the Gospels and follow Christ's mysteries in that

> wonderful cycle established by the Church herself in the liturgical cycle from Advent to Pentecost.[25]

But then, in the *second* place, Christ is the author of our redemption, the infinitely spacious treasure house of grace itself —
not simply its living portrait. Thanks to the personal union of
divinity and humanity in the Word, his efforts on our behalf
have an inexhaustible efficacy, and this is true above all of his
crowning action for us: the voluntary self-substitution whereby
the stainless Victim won for us not just the privilege but the *right*
of eternal life with God.

But if this be common doctrine, Marmion's distinctive contribution appears more largely in the *third* Christological perspective
he offers. Christ is our spiritual life, *acting* in the soul's sanctuary so
as to help us, on the basis of his merits, to imitate him:

> For certain souls, the life of Christ Jesus is one subject of
> meditation among others; this is not enough. Christ is not
> one of the means of spiritual life; he is all our spiritual life.[26]

What of the Holy Spirit? Life in Christ is precisely access to
the Spirit:

> The Holy Spirit renders holy the being and activity of Christ;
> and because, in Christ, this holiness attains the supreme
> degree, because all human holiness is to be modeled upon
> it and must be subject to it, the Church sings daily: *Tu solus
> sanctus, Jesu Christe.*[27]

Everything else Marmion has to say — about the Church, Our
Lady, the communion of saints, the sacraments, and meditation and
prayer — is guided and governed by these central insights into the
mystery of salvation as supernatural divine adoption in Jesus Christ.

Love of the Liturgy

The secret of his success was that *in the Liturgy* wise theology and sound doctrine had *become* prayer. The sheer objectivity of divine revelation — with Jesus Christ at its heart as the source of all perfections, since he is the source of all grace — could be reproduced in an objective spirituality by this very means.

Despite the catholicity of his source material, after the Bible the Liturgy was paramount. On Scripture he remarked:

> The principal source of prayer is to be found in Holy Scripture read with devotion and laid up in the heart.[28]

But on the Office — much of it, of course, itself biblical — he said:

> Those who recite the Divine Office with generosity and recollection easily arrive at contemplation.[29]

And as to the Liturgy of the sacraments, here, too, he saw how only a contemplative attitude could draw from the mysteries their full potential. We should look to the heavenly Father with Christ, asking him to renew in us all that the Church herself has asked for us and wrought in us at the reception of the sacraments.

For Marmion, the Liturgy is grounded in the Holy Trinity, and more specifically in the Son's own being as praise of the Father:

> By the very fact of being what he is, the Eternal Word is like a Divine canticle, a living canticle, singing the praise of the Father, expressing the plenitude of his perfections.[30]

This is the "canticle" that began to be sung on earth — when the Word became incarnate, and "associated all humanity, by right and in principle" in this perfect praise.[31] After the example of her Bridegroom, and by communion with him, the Church offers a sacrifice of praise to the eternal Father. Her Liturgy is *vox Sponsae,* the "voice of the Bride." (Marmion's favorite title for the Church was *Sponsa Verbi,* the "Spouse of the Word."[32])

All the prayers of the Church end, so Marmion points out, with some version of the words *per Christum Dominum nostrum* ("through Christ our Lord"):

> Christ being united to the Church gives her his power of adoring and praising God. The Church is united to Jesus and leans upon him.[33]

Her dowry is not only "her miseries, her weakness." It is also "her heart to love with and her lips with which to praise." But for his part, the Bridegroom brings to her "his satisfactions, his merits, his precious Blood, all his riches." And by way of spiritual interpretation of the *Song of Songs* (8:5), Marmion hears the words of Solomon — "Who is this who cometh up from the desert, flowing with delights, leaning upon her Beloved?" (Douay Version) — as a wondering exclamation of the angels in their contemplation of Christ's Mystical Body as she offers his own homage to the adorable Trinity.[34] This is powerful intercession indeed, since, as one with the prayer of the Word Incarnate, it cannot but be heard. We note how, for Marmion, praise itself is intercession, and there is no better intercession than praise. This is unusual doctrine, and it derives, as we shall see, from the primacy of doxology in the Christian life. For Marmion, everything in that life must be interpreted from the standpoint of giving God praise.

Marmion now goes on to say that the praise the Church offers in the Mass and the Divine Office has not only intercessory potency but sanctifying value as well. We have already seen how for him Christ, in the various mysteries of his life, is the exemplary cause of our salvation. So it will not surprise us to learn that, according to Marmion, the explanation for this "sanctifying value" of the Liturgy lies in the annual liturgical cycle, whereby the Church lays out the mysteries of Christ for our loving contemplation:

> The Church not only gives us, each year, a living representation of the life of her Bridegroom, but she makes us penetrate as far as the creature is able to penetrate into the soul of Christ so that, reading his inmost dispositions, we may share them and be more intimately united to our Divine Head. The Church, with profound art and wonderful ease, helps us to fulfil the precept of St Paul, 'Let this mind be in you which was in Christ Jesus' (Philippians 2, 5).[35]

This has the effect, adds Marmion, of actualizing in us the elective grace whereby the Father wills that we should be "in" the Beloved. In his words, it "fulfils the rule of our predestination."

With full-blooded supernatural realism, Marmion insists that these mysteries are not just a matter of historical record. (The Crucifixion, for example, is not appropriately signaled by the words of Mrs. Alexander's hymn, "There is a green hill far away.") As he writes: "These mysteries of Christ that the Church causes us to celebrate each year are *still living mysteries*."[36] Their virtue remains inexhaustible; and through their celebration in the Church's Liturgy, Christ "makes faithful souls ['according to the measure of our faith'] partakers of the graces these mysteries contain."[37] In the cycles that find their culmination at Christmas and Easter, the prayer of the Church is a "sure way for us":

> We could not take one that would lead us more directly to Christ, and make our life more one with his.[38]

Nor was this liturgiocentric viewpoint in any way narrow. Marmion did not neglect the wider, if more diffuse, sacramentality of the world. He loved the *Benedicite*, the Bible's own Canticle of the Creatures, for this reason — its wondering praise at the creation and especially the human goodness that is creation's crown.

As more and more "lights" on the Word Incarnate were given him, Marmion came to see the whole of life in doxological terms. By a perpetual "Glory to the Father," we honor the Father as font of the whole Godhead and the entire world besides, laying before him our plans and desires so that the initiative in our lives may be his. By just this dependence on the Father, we imitate the only-begotten Son, who proceeds from the Father, and always thought, desired, and acted in an absolute dependence on his Source. In so doing, we sing an abiding "Glory be to the Holy Spirit," the living Love whereby, through the Son, we return to the Father as our last end. And finally, all this is a "Glory be to the Son" himself, because we worship the Son by joining ourselves with him in his acceptance — for himself, and for his members, the Church — of the will of the Father in its completeness.[39]

In an age such as our own, when spirituality too often sinks in a morass of psychotherapy and sentiment, Blessed Columba Marmion's exultation in the sheer objectivity of the divine plan, life, and nature makes him a needed prophet for the times. But it is his love of the Liturgy — to the point that we can see in him how all existence can become "doxological," lived for God's praise and glory — that most moves those who venerate him.

THREE

Great Heart
Gilbert Keith Chesterton and the Love of the Virtues

Introduction

Emile Cammaerts, in his early study of Chesterton, praised him with these words:

> He was indeed brilliant, in the sense that he made the Christian virtues shine with the sparkle of his wit, and covered the corresponding vices with contumely.[40]

Commending the virtues — both human and Christian, natural and supernatural, in their breathtakingly full range — came equally first on Chesterton's list of priorities. Equally first, that is to say, with his other main preoccupation, which was showing Catholic Christianity to be as wide as — nay, wider than — the world.[41] Putting these two concerns together, we can say this: If ever Chesterton is beatified, it should surely be under the title "Gilbert the Greathearted."

Chesterton's appreciation of the faith is a lucid appreciation of something essentially variegated. It also conveys a commitment that is tenaciously strong and penetratingly deep. Such appreciation is customarily thought of as "liberal"; such commitment is generally treated as "conservative." In Chesterton, they go together.

To Chesterton's eyes, for the faith to be multifaceted, faith is the opposite of its being protean, amorphous, elusive, or ever-shifting. After all, the hardest naturally occurring substance — diamond — is often multifaceted as well:

> The Faith faces every possible way, so far as angle and attitude to life is concerned, and there is no artistic style it cannot use. The jewel has a hundred facets, and reflects every color and corner of the sky; but that does not mean that it wavers or wobbles; and those who would break it find it the hardest stone in the world.[42]

The metaphor changes from solids to liquids when he adds that the purer the orthodox faith, the more inspirational its power:

> Again and again, before our time, men have grown content with a diluted doctrine. And again and again there has followed on that dilution, coming as out of the darkness in a crimson cataract, the strength of the red original wine.[43]

In this, the Catholic religion is not just divinely desirable. It is happily human as well:

> Man can be defined as an animal that makes dogmas. As he piles doctrine on doctrine and conclusion on conclusion in the formation of some tremendous scheme of philosophy and religion, he is, in the only legitimate sense of which the expression is capable, becoming more and more human. When he drops one doctrine after another in a refined skepticism, when he declines to tie himself to a system, when he says that he has outgrown definitions, when, in his own

imagination, he sits as God, holding no form of creed but contemplating all, then he is by that very process sinking slowly backwards into the vagueness of the vagrant animals and the unconsciousness of the grass. Trees have no dogmas. Turnips are singularly broad-minded.[44]

Some Biographical Lights

Whence did this paragon of lay theological understanding arise? He was born in the same year as Marmion, 1874, into a highly literate middle-class household in Kensington — then, as now, a socially desirable London borough. His mother, of mixed Scottish and Swiss-French origin, gave him his wittiness, but not her somewhat bullying attitude to people. His father, whom he resembled more, was a dreamy, somewhat ineffectual person, who was fortunately able to leave the affairs of the family business — they were estate agents, or what in America are known as Realtors — in more capable hands. Edward Chesterton passed on to his elder son his huge store of English poetry learned by heart, as well as his favorite hobbies: drawing and painting, designing toy theaters, and magic lanterns. The home was a cell of good living:

> The old-fashioned Englishman, like my father, sold houses
> for a living but filled his own house with his life.[45]

The gangly, absentminded Gilbert at first got poor marks at the academically prestigious St. Paul's School; but gradually, not least through its debating societies and schoolboy reviews, perceptive masters began to realize they had on their hands a wayward genius. This would be the verdict of many of his contemporaries, though "wayward" would change to "lovable if (or because) erratic." He was not cut out for standard scholarship.

So much became apparent at University College, London, while his teachers at the Slade School of Art (where he took concurrent classes in art training) soon realized that further time spent there would only undermine a style of drawing he had already mastered. (Had he written nothing, he would still have become celebrated as one of the great illustrators of the English book, using extraordinary economy of means.) It was at the Slade that he encountered, and felt the full force of, *fin-de-siècle* decadence, amoralism, and even diabolism — all of which caused a severe personal crisis, but also made possible, by way of reason, the working out of his own metaphysics of morals.

Chesterton's life is easily told, since it only has three significant events: his becoming a journalist in the old Fleet Street; his marriage (he was devoted, though his wife was frail and, for physiological reasons on her side, it is likely the marriage was never consummated); and his entry into the Catholic Church.

Chesterton's journalism was that of a shining knight. He was Mr. Passionate for Truth. He entered the trade just before it became the plaything of proprietor-magnates, whose writers had to mind their ideological p's and q's. That older journalism was an excellent training for a writer with an intellectual mission to the public. He devised a forceful personal style, based on unusual parallels and striking juxtapositions, and a rich resourcefulness in literary tropes. (He is still a marvelous read, even if sometimes the "paradoxes" come too thick and fast, and the metaphors can be overblown.) This he put at the service of a coherent set of humane convictions, which hardly wavered whether the occasion of his writing were the introduction of divorce legislation, Charles Dickens, Michelangelo, or the South African War. His commissioned works on literary and artistic figures, while full of insight (if also, as he unrepentantly admitted, inaccurate on points of detail), do not really differ in manner or message from the newspaper and magazine articles whose subjects he had chosen himself and collected together in book form. They are an education in wisdom, and so — as Edwardian intellectuals like George Bernard Shaw and H. G. Wells, by taking them seriously, admitted — they are "philosophy" in the best sense of that word.

Much of the suffering, as well as the solace, in Chesterton's life came through his wife, Frances. Frances Chesterton never seemed to recover from the tragic early motoring accident that took the life of her sister Gertrude (Rudyard Kipling's secretary) and the loss of her brother — who was also deeply affected by Gertrude's death — through suicide. It was, however, and remained a marriage filled with love. Without Frances, the remarkably disorganized Chesterton would never have managed his mammoth schedule of lecturing and writing. At the time of his breakdown in 1914, brought on by overwork and, it must be said, excessive indulgence in food and drink (his physical size put a huge strain on his heart), her devoted nursing pulled him through.

That was also the moment when, herself a devout Anglican, she began, at least, to withdraw her opposition to his entering the Catholic Church. Chesterton himself said later that he became a Catholic out of his need for absolution. To some, this has seemed a strange rationale for conversion. His amiability was proverbial, and his lack of malice unusual among intellectuals. He conveyed to others a refreshing sense of moral innocence. But at the Slade, he had known demons in the heart. And as a professional commentator on social facts, at home and abroad, he scarcely lacked evidence of the turpitude of humankind.

Some of Chesterton's most "Catholic" writing was done before he became a Catholic. The best of the "Father Brown" stories, "The Blue Cross," was written as an Anglican. He composed

Orthodoxy before the form of Christianity he embraced was fully orthodox. But his reconciliation with Rome in 1922 enlarged the cosmopolitanism of his very English outlook — as well as the range of his lecture tours! In 1926, shortly after their silver wedding anniversary, he had the joy of seeing his wife follow him. Ten years of life remained to them together. Devastated, she survived him by just two years, after his death in 1936.

The Need for Chesterton

Our time needs Chesterton as much as did his own. The reason, identified by Dr. John Coates in his study of GKC as cultural critic, lies in the crying need he can satisfy, which is a "pondered theory of the good."[46] Chesterton realized that no civilization can flourish unless it is underpinned by the virtues. Their flourishing is what gives us, here and now (short of God, then), the human good. A civilization worthy of man has a *moral structure*, whose character turns on human nature itself. No spirituality that does justice to the human can ignore this.

In the first of the "masters" considered in this book, we saw how Erich Przywara presented Thérèse of Lisieux as the Catholic Christian answer to Nietzsche. Likewise, A. R. Orage, editor of *New Age*, that major player among Edwardian journals, was converted from his Nietzschean view of man-in-constant-evolution-toward-superman by pondering the message of Chesterton. Specifically, what became evident to him was the truth of Chesterton's thesis that much of the crisis of modernity stems from our unwillingness to recognize the *definiteness* of the human species and, as a result, the related definiteness that belongs to our nature's native good:

> Starting from a false conception of the nature of man, the mind continually sees everything in a false light. Its whole

object is to become something that it really is not, and can
never be . . . with human nature undefined, nothing else is
definable.[47]

Natural and Supernatural Virtues

In this, it is not enough to be *mere* humanists. In the first place,
we may well need divine revelation so as to study our grasp of the
human first principles. In *Orthodoxy*, Chesterton wrote:

> The chief mark and element of insanity is reason used with-
> out root, reason in the void. The man who begins to think
> without the proper first principles goes mad, the man who
> begins to think at the wrong end.[48]

But then, in the second place, in the "concrete" divine economy of creation and salvation, our human nature is ordered toward a superhuman goal, such that the only way the good of our
nature can actually be achieved is now *super*natural. As Chesterton put it in *The Thing*:

> For Catholics it is a fundamental dogma of the Faith that
> all human beings, without any exception whatever, are
> specially made, were specially shaped and pointed like shin-
> ing arrows, for the end of hitting the mark of Beatitude.[49]

And for that reason, then, to do justice to our humanity in
its very root, we need the moral virtues that Christendom has
identified on the basis of the historic divine revelation. For if
there *is* a superhuman good (and much concerning the human
situation is unintelligible without positing some goal beyond our

natural inheritance), the features of that good can, by definition, only be made known in a superhuman way.

While Chesterton did not deny that aspects of our historical patrimony need renewal and reform, he held that renewal and reform are a matter of clearing the grime off the beautiful image of man *already given us* by revelation. As he wrote in *The Thing*:

> We need a rally of the really human things; will which is morals, memory which is tradition, culture which is the mental thrift of our fathers. And here humanism cannot substitute for superhumanism. The modern world, with its modern movement, is living on Catholic capital. It is using, and using up, the truths that remain to it out of the old treasury of Christendom, including of course many truths known to pagan antiquity but crystallised in Christendom.[50]

The Unity of the Virtues

Spirituality, like culture itself, requires not this or that isolated virtue but the full configuration of all the virtues that count — which means all the virtues, "period" (as Americans say). It is only when we see the virtues together, and in the round, that we glimpse that constellation of good dispositions which properly belongs to our determinate nature *en route* to its beatitude. And without the Christian revelation, that is no longer plain.

To name the virtues, we must list them singly; nonetheless, they do not, in their *ensemble*, simply add up to a catalog. Rather, they make up a pattern, an ordered totality, what the Swiss dogmatician Hans Urs von Balthasar would call a *Gestalt*, a significant form. To cite from *The Thing* again:

Humanism may try to pick up the pieces [i.e., the individual virtues]; but can it stick them together? Where is the cement which made religion corporate and popular, which can prevent it falling to pieces in a debris of individualistic tasks and degrees? What is to prevent one Humanist wanting chastity without humility, and another humility without chastity, and another truth or beauty without either? The problem of an enduring ethic and culture consists in finding an arrangement of the pieces by which they remain related, as do the stones arranged in an arch. And I know only one scheme that has thus proved its solidity, bestriding lands and ages with its gigantic arches and carrying everywhere the high river of baptism upon an aqueduct of Rome.[51]

That passage is cited from a late work, when Chesterton had left Anglo-Catholicism behind and discovered, with Petrine communion, the thought of St. Thomas Aquinas, in whose ethics the idea of the unity of the virtues plays an important role. But long before he opened the *Summa Theologiae*, Chesterton had grasped the *composed* character of the good that civilization needs. Already, in his work *Orthodoxy*, he had this to say:

The modern world is not evil; in some ways the modern world is far too good. It is full of wild and wasted virtues. When a religious scheme is shattered (as Christianity was shattered by the Reformation), it is not merely the vices that are let loose. The vices are, indeed, let loose, and they wander and do damage. But the virtues are let loose also: and the virtues do more terrible damage. The modern world is full of the old Christian virtues gone mad. The virtues have gone mad because they have been isolated from each other and are wandering alone. Thus some scientists care for truth; and their truth is pitiless. Thus some humanitarians only care for pity; and their pity (I am sorry to say) is often untruthful.[52]

It would not mislead to say that throughout his life Chesterton was seeking how the mutual perfecting of the virtues might be possible. He was trying to discern — and succeeding in discerning — the structure of virtuous living that is spirituality's precondition and undertow. In *Orthodoxy*, he speaks of this structure as "an exact and perilous balance, like that of a desperate romance" and again as no

mere victory of some one thing swallowing up everything else, love or pride or peace or adventure; it must be a definite picture composed of these elements in their best proportion and relation.[53]

Perhaps the most striking statement of this Chestertonian project of pointing up the human good as a structured whole comes in GKC's study of Chaucer. There he takes up the idea of harmonious equilibrium into a more mobile and flowing simile, the simile of the "dance" of the virtues — a dance which has for its center a unique still point in the turning world, a revelation of the ultimately Christological character of the human good, of Christ as the true midpoint of culture:

Medieval morality was full of the idea that one thing must balance another, that each stood on one side or the other of something that was in the middle, and something remained in the middle. There might be any amount of movement, but it was movement round this central thing; perpetually altering the attitudes, but preserving the balance. The virtues were like children going round the Mulberry Bush, only the Mulberry Bush was that Burning Bush which they made symbolical of the Incarnation; that flamboyant bush in which the Virgin and Child appear in the picture, with René of Provence and his beloved wife kneeling on either side. Now since that break in history, whatever we call it or whatever we think of it, the Dance has turned into a Race. That is, the dancers lose their balance and only recover it by running towards some object, or alleged object; not an object within their circle or their possession, but an object which they do not yet possess. It is a flying object, a disappearing object.

Chesterton insists that he is not now concerned with "condemning or commending the religion of the Race or the religion of the Dance. I am only pointing out that this is the fundamental difference between them. One is rhythmic and recurrent movement, because there is a known center; while the other is precipitate or progressive movement, because there is an unknown goal" — something which Chesterton links with the accelerating pace of modern life by which standard "the Canterbury pilgrims do not seem to be in a very great hurry to get to Canterbury."[54]

As the invocation of Nicolas Froment's late-fifteenth-century triptych "The Burning Bush" (it is in the Cathedral of St. Sauveur at Aix en Provence) should indicate to us, all of this is, in Chesterton's mind, inextricably bound up with the existence of God, God as goal of human nature and history.

One could go so far as to say, indeed, that it constitutes a virtual demonstration of the knowability to the human mind of the Creator Lord, as what the First Vatican Council called our true *finis*, our real end. For if we are being led to a complex yet unified good, to a *composed* good, this cannot be by "an impersonal force." It can only be, as Chesterton writes in *Orthodoxy*, by the agency of a *personal* God who alone could prepare "a city with just streets and architectural proportions" — a differentiated yet ultimately unitary fulfillment nicely adjusted to all the aspects of our nature as a whole.[55]

Some Crucial Virtues

Chesterton commends a wonderful range of virtues in the course of his work. Indeed, comparing Chesterton's celebration of the virtues to the great carvings found in the porches of the French Gothic cathedrals or the frescoes of the Arena Chapel in Padua, Cammaerts proposed that this "great company" of the virtues were GKC's *real* subject. Surveying them all is quite a task, some part of which I have attempted elsewhere.[56] Here I would like to draw attention to a crucial few.

In a manner all his own, Chesterton combined the virtues of the "Little Way"[57] — humility, simplicity, and innocence — with a virtue we might wish to associate more with Marmion in the grand sweep of his liturgically-centered dogmatic vision, and that is the virtue of *festivity*. The virtues of littleness — what in *Orthodoxy* Chesterton calls "modesty" — have suffered dislocation. Modesty "has moved from the organ of ambition to the organ of conviction where it was never meant to be." The equipoise of the virtues is only struck when modesty — that is, simplicity, innocence, and humility — in the organ of ambition is balanced by celebratory sumptuousness in the organ of conviction. And the key to the virtue of festivity is placed within our grasp when we hear how

> we need so to view the world as to combine an idea of wonder and an idea of welcome.[58]

Thanks to festivity, we see and celebrate in our lives both the unfamiliar (applauded by wonder) and the familiar (saluted by welcome). And this gives Catholic spirituality its typical combination of excitement and reassurance. This, so Chesterton says, "Christendom has rightly named romance."[59]

Conclusion

The admiration and praise that wonder and welcome call forth bring us in conclusion to that Burning Bush — the Word Incarnate — which in *Chaucer* Chesterton saw as the focalizing center of the dance of the virtues. At the end of his study of that fourteenth-century "maker," Chesterton returns to the Christological midpoint when in a wonderful passage he describes the cultured man, Chaucer, as appareled in Jesus Christ:

> Between the black robes of Gower and the grey gown of Langland he stands clothed in scarlet like all the household of love; and emblazoned with the Sacred Heart.[60]

But Chesterton's ground for this encomium is the *charity* that, he maintains, soaked Chaucer's poetic sensibility. Like St. Thomas Aquinas, though not in his vocabulary, Chesterton ends by lauding the virtue of charity as the form of all these assembled virtues, the structure which gives them, natural or supernatural, their true vindication and proper role:

Chaucer had the one thing needful; he had the frame of
mind that is the ultimate result of right reason and a universal philosophy; the temper that is the flower and fruit of
all the tillage and the toil of moralists and theologians. He
had Charity; that is the heart and not merely the mind of
our ancient Christendom.

Here all the virtues come together, not least the natural ones,
for this was

the shout that showed that normality had been found. For
a great voice was given by God, and a great volume of sing-
ing, not to his saints who deserved it much better . . . but
only suddenly, and for a season, to the most human of human beings.[61]

But if charity structures all the virtues, then the culture that
the moral life structures in its turn can only be what the post-
conciliar popes Paul VI and John Paul II have sought: in their
phrase, a "civilization of love."

Chesterton cleaved to the view that, by carrying the Gospel
and the life of the Incarnation, the Church enjoys a culture-trans-
forming power, a power to reassemble the pieces of the lost unity
of the moral pattern of culture, and so enable human beings to
flourish in all those places where they interrelate and where their
manifold needs and enthusiasms are pursued. With the still-Angli-
can Ronald Knox, Chesterton considered, on the one hand, that

Unbelievers . . . want definition not accommodation. 'The
modern Church is like a cozy doctor saying, "Tell us what
you want to believe and we will see about it" '.[62]

On the other hand, Chesterton did profoundly believe in the unique congruence of the faith with human nature. If people *really* knew what they wanted to believe, would they not fall on the Gospel with a glad cry?

FOUR

Poet of Faith
Charles Péguy and the Love of Hope

Introduction

"Hope" may seem an odd thing to love; but if, as we saw with Chesterton, one can "love" the virtues, one can surely love the theological virtue of hope. And the ills of the soul to which theological hope is the antidote are among the most widespread in the modern world and Church, as well as the most mortal. To explore the work of Charles Péguy is to discover a spiritual physician who can inoculate successfully against typically modern diseases of the soul.

Péguy the Man

Who was he? Born at Orléans in 1873, into a family only recently emerged from the peasantry, he was a would-be academic turned poet, essayist, and dramatist. To the political classes in France, he was, above all, the editor of the "Fortnightly Review," *Les Cahiers de la Quinzaine*: a journal, briefly influential during the "Dreyfus Affair," a struggle for justice for a Jewish army officer wrongly accused of treason, which polarized the nation. *Les Cahiers* represented his unique brand of moral astringency, social criticism, and religious thought.

To the Catholic searching out sources of spirituality, Péguy was this and much more.

Owing to his father's early death and his mother's consequent need to support her family by productive work (she was a — highly successful — chair caner), Péguy was brought up by his grandmother, an illiterate whose effortless rooting in an older France, more humane and Christian than that of the Third Republic, would affect him for life. At his Catholic primary school, he learned more about God and the saints of France. At his state secondary school, a teacher identified him as outstandingly gifted and arranged for a scholarship. The point of this was to enable him to prepare for the examinations for the prestigious École Normale Supérieure, the Parisian training ground for the professorial corps of the French universities.

At about the age of twenty, he became an unbeliever, an anticlerical, and an ardent — if utopian — socialist. The reasons for this seismic shift in fundamental allegiance have never really been clarified. They are likely to have involved, first, the Church's rejection of universalism (and hence her teaching that everlasting punishment is a reality), and secondly, the feebleness of Catholic efforts to alleviate proletarian misery, which he could witness in various parts of industrialized north-central France.

The liberal bourgeoisie who mostly ran the France of the Third Republic need not have lost any sleep over the revolutionary threat posed by the *Amis de la cour rose* ("Friends of the rose court"): Péguy and his friends working for socialism in a fashion "more like that of St. Francis than of Karl Marx."[63] In 1896, Péguy took a year out from the École on the pretext that his eyes were giving him trouble (he would never return). He had learned typography. He married (not, unfortunately, happily) and used his wife's dowry to set up a small socialist bookshop and printing venture, which soon came to economic grief. He published not only his visionary picture of the perfect society — *Marcel, pre-*

mier dialogue de la cité harmonieuse — but also his first poetic study of St. Joan of Arc. He presented a socialistic St. Joan (though much of the historical detail was otherwise correct), but a Joan with enough premodern religious virtue to suggest that he was unlikely to remain a secularist for long.

His disillusionment with the Socialist Party (though not his own social vision) intensified, under the shock of a party resolution forbidding internal criticism and the announcement by its leader, Jaurès, that strike action (notably in munitions) would be mounted if there were armed resistance to a German invasion. The philosophical writings of Henri Bergson (a Jewish convert to Catholicism) — with their spirited defense of the reality of the soul, of freedom, and of divine creation — reawakened his religious convictions. The latter melded with those commitments on which he had never wavered: a detestation of materialism, scientism, and the worship of money, as well as his love of *la France ancienne* ("the old France") — at once pious and ribald, courageous, and hardworking — of his grandmother's memories and tales. Even though the unyielding opposition of his wife (after his death, she was to become a Catholic herself) prevented him from having his children baptized and returning to sacramental practice, he declared himself a son of the Church, and his subsequent writings gave that claim no lie. As we shall see, perhaps their greatest theme is hope. As an American critic has put it, linking Péguy in this respect with his longer-lived contemporary Paul Claudel:

> In their imaginative evocations of the past both found renewal for the present . . . and with it, Hope. This rediscovery is what gives to the work of each poet its vitality, its germinal quality. For, of the three Virtues — Faith, Hope,

Charity — if Charity is the greatest, surely Hope in today's
world is the most difficult to practice.[64]

After his conversion (or re-conversion), Péguy's *Cahiers* found
targets in such gurus of secular, positivist France as Hippolyte
Taine and Ernest Renan. The contempt for the (pagan and) Christian past so clearly entertained by scientism, the "irreligion of the
future," opened the vials of his wrath:

> It awoke his most profound mistrust to consign his beloved
> past to the limbo of things outworn, to hold up his cher-
> ished heroes and saints of the French tradition to the mock-
> eries of historical criticism, to let man's reach so infinitely
> exceed his grasp in a cosmos both un-French and unclassi-
> cal, and to hold that the great rhythms of history had ceased
> and the age of consolidation and fulfilment come. The no-
> tion that modern man is the crown and summit of life —
> this, surely, was the oldest heresy in history.[65]

Péguy set out to show that there was more real power of rejuvenation in the saints — *la sainteté agissante* ("sanctity acting"),
incarnate and efficacious, in history — than in the cold manipu-
lators of modern social control, and this thanks to *the* Incarnation, when the Word became flesh and joined our dear fleshly
world to his eternally youthful divine life.

This is the theme of his mature poetic output, the various
"Mysteries" (*mystères*) and "Tapestries" (*tapisseries*), by which he
celebrated the salvation history of Scripture and the lives of the
saints against its backdrop in man's historical experience at large.

I wrote "man" there, but of capital importance in Péguy's
Christian vision of history is woman. The key female figures are

not history's "scientific" muse, Clio (whom he portrays as forever indecisively consulting an enormous card index system), but Eve and Mary (our natural mother and our mother by grace, respectively). Possibly his finest poetic achievement is the eighty-line quatrains of his "Presentation of Beauce [the countryside around Paris] to Our Lady of Chartres," written in thanksgiving for the birth of his son, and commemorating the two pilgrimages he made on foot, from Paris to Chartres, in 1912 and 1913. Nor is it surprising that the Mother of the Word Incarnate should have elicited such supreme beauty in language since, for Péguy, her Son is the meeting place of earth and heaven, when an arch is built, one span of which rises up from the soil of Israel and the other is let down from the divine Trinity above.

He had never thought he would live to be fifty. And so it proved.

On August 1, 1914, Germany and France found themselves at war — the war that Péguy, like many other observers of the Wilhelmine Reich, had believed would come. On August 4, he joined his regiment and moved off into Lorraine. On September 5, in a field near Meaux, in the early stages of the Battle of the Marne, as he was shouting orders to his men, a German bullet found its target:

> Happy are they who, under the gaze of God,
> die for the 'terre charnelle', marry her blood
> to theirs, and, in strange Christian hope, go down
> into the darkness of resurrection,
>
> into sap, ragwort, melancholy thistle,
> almondy meadowsweet, the freshet-brook
> rising and running through small wilds of oak,
> past the elder-tump that is the child's castle.[66]

In these words, and in the entire poem of which they form part, an English poet renders critical yet marveling homage to a French poet.

Péguy's Message

His message is both positive and negative — but it is more positive than negative because it is founded on a hope that is not simply a human hope but a *theological* hope, the hope that springs from a hope-filled God.

Péguy hates the triviality of much in modern life, its moral and aesthetic ugliness, the myopia that results from bracketing out revelation and the sacred. But he does not consider any man bound by these restrictions. Thanks to Bergson, he never lost the sense that determinism, whether biological or social, is false. Thanks to Bergson again, he acquired the sense that qualitatively real time (*la durée*), as distinct from mere quantitative clock time, links past and future in a present which opens on them both and on the eternity that is their common ground. While the twentieth-century Church has seen plenty of "opening to the world" that dissolves Christianity into secular modernity, it can, healthfully, contemplate in Péguy someone who climbed up from out of the modern world into the realm of Christian grace.

Péguy's Poem on Hope

One way to do that is via his great poem on hope, *The Porch of the Mystery of the Second Virtue*. The reference is of course to the three theological virtues, in whose trio hope appears in the middle, flanked by faith on one side and charity on the other.

In his poem, Péguy makes two general points about the virtue of hope. First, among the three theological virtues — these dispositions that we know of from divine revelation, and experience personally through the grace that accompanies the reception of revelation in our own lives — hope is a neglected virtue, a little girl hidden behind her more imposing sisters. Secondly, hope is not simply a virtue. It is also, says Péguy, a mystery. It is a way of speaking about the whole plan of God for our salvation and indeed about the God of salvation himself. Few virtues can claim to attain the status of a mystery — comparable to the mystery of the Incarnation or the Atonement, truths about God in his relation to us that are so inexhaustible that we will never come to the end of them. Hope can be both of these things because it is a way of understanding God's gracious revelation of himself and his attitudes toward us in Jesus Christ and by the power of his Spirit.

Péguy's poem opens with the arresting words, "The faith that I love best," says God, "is hope." As his American translator comments on *The Porch*'s opening stanzas:

> God wishes to be glorified in every aspect of creation, but he is best glorified in the virtue of hope, for it is in hope that a person expresses most profoundly the greatest trust in God, the greatest confidence in God's love.[67]

Péguy makes God shrug his shoulders at the thought of faith. There is so much evidence for God's existence and for the truth of God Incarnate that the fact of people believing is hardly a cause for comment. And as for charity — given the way the Son suffered for love of sinners — people would have to have hearts of stone *not* to love their neighbors. But what God finds really astonishing (says Péguy, taking poetic license) is that Christians live by hope in him. As the divine voice comments:

. . . my grace must indeed be an incredible force
and must flow freely and like an inexhaustible river
since the first time it flowed and since it has forever been
    flowing
in my natural and supernatural creation.[68]

Hope gives the Christian life its form. To live the Christian life is to treat existence as a gift from a Giver in whom hope is never misplaced. Péguy speaks of the Christian as a child who, in absolute dependence on his parent, "smiles inwardly" because he enjoys the complete assurance of being at all times carried by the parent's love. Every rational creature who is able to live thus, from out of the gift of hope, becomes a witness to the triumph of God's grace — and therefore leads God to marvel at his own glory: "My grace must indeed be great."

The Hope-filled God

So far, however, Péguy has not justified the claim of his title that hope is a mystery — one of those inexhaustible truths about God's own being and action that he revealed to us through Scripture read in Tradition. *Can* hope be a truth about God himself? Péguy thinks so, because the God of Scripture is an expectant, a hope-filled God, who awaits with eager longing the return of his children to himself. Making hope an attribute of God is a thoroughly audacious move. Yet the witness of revelation is that the God who in no ordinary sense can *need* anything at all, not even the entirety of his creation, does in some extraordinary sense *long* for it — long for us — such that this love-longing of God for us is the primary presupposition of the whole story of salvation. Péguy means this to be a truth we can profitably contemplate for the rest of our lives, and also a stimulus to changing the direction of those lives and making them more fruitful for the good of all the Church.

But first of all, the focus is on *changing* them, because the revelation of the hope of God is meant to create hope in us. As Péguy writes:

> You must have confidence in God, he certainly has had
>   confidence in us.
> You must trust God, he has certainly put his trust
>   in us.
> You must hope in God, he has certainly hoped in us.
> You must give God a chance, he has certainly given us a
>   chance.
> What chance?
> Every chance.
> You must have faith in God, he has certainly had faith
>   in us.[69]

But then, secondly, the revelation of the hope-filled God whose grace elicits hope in us is intended to make our lives fruitful in activity that will assist his Church to spread his Word in the world. Péguy does not know whether to laugh or cry when he thinks how God has made the communication of his Gospel depend on our frail selves — who are also, however, the elect that is his Church:

> We perishable creations, perishable creatures,
> once created, once born, once baptised,
> . . . what unfortunately depends on us, fortunately,
> one after the other, is to nourish the living word,
> to nourish for a time the eternal word,

after so many others, before so many others,
ever since it was uttered,
until the threshold of Judgment Day.[70]

Just as the faithful, as they enter church, pass each other holy water from the stoup (that, incidentally, was a favored ecclesiological image of Cardinal Congar's), so:

Like a relay,
In the same hope, the word of God is passed on.[71]

Hence, Elizabeth received its presence from Mary.

Hope for Eternity

What, then, in our prayer and our action are we to hope for? First, and foremost, the bliss of enjoying with others the life of God as his friends. As St. Thomas Aquinas explains, by the virtue of hope we actively regard that goal as something possible of attainment through the help of God:

> The good we should rightly and chiefly hope for from God is an unlimited one, matching the power of God who helps us. Such a good is life eternal, consisting in the joyful possession of God himself. This is simply to say that we should hope for nothing less from God than his very self; his goodness, by which he confers good upon creaturely things, is nothing less than his own being. And so the proper and principal object of hope is indeed eternal blessedness.[72]

Compared with this perfectly possible goal, writes St. Thomas, we should count all obstacles as naught:

To one who sets his heart upon something great, anything less is of minor importance. And so the man hoping for everlasting bliss is not inclined to count anything else as difficult when measured against this hope.[73]

Hope for Christendom

But does this mean, then, that Péguy was wrong to hope for all the other things with which *The Portal of the Mystery of Hope* is concerned: the continuation and flourishing of Christendom, for instance; or the survival from one generation to another of the parishes of France; or, we ourselves might say, come to that, of England?[74] Not at all. St. Thomas is making the point that, unless our lives are thoroughly centered on God and eternal life with him in his Kingdom, it is not likely that we shall accomplish any great work for him on earth. But he by no means discourages us from hoping — with the theological virtue of hope, of course — for other ends as well, so long as these are seen in their ordering toward that same eternal beatitude.

Now it is manifest that the flourishing and — yes, let us dare use the word, politically incorrect though it is — the *triumph* of that Mother Church which preexisted in Mary is directly ordered to the enjoyment of everlasting bliss by the greatest possible number of people; for it is by the faith, the sacraments, and the intercession of the Church that the Word Incarnate proposes to save men and women on earth.

St. Thomas explains that we can sin against such hope in two ways. One is by supposing that God can go back on his covenanted Word and save people quite as efficaciously by other means, as he would do were he to bring them to the waters of Baptism and the Holy Catholic Church by which the economies of the Son and the Spirit are visibly embodied. The other way is to cease to expect a share in the divine goodness in the Age to Come and consequently to abandon the effort to bring others to share in that fulfillment by offering them the Christian faith in its plenary form; this is despair. Péguy tells us we must never relax our vigilance in either direction.

Living From the Incarnation

The Incarnation is the moment when time opens out onto that which liberates time and justifies time, making time "all right." All human life can be renewed and begin again because it can always draw on the eternal that is now present in it with fullest force. The temporality of the human world now lies open to an eternity that seeks to transfigure it.

To neglect this new relation to the eternal is to condemn ourselves to always getting things in some way wrong, to making a false calculation of possibilities, giving a false audit of human prospects. By this new relation, the human realm has ceased to be a closed domain where everything off-limits can be treated by the rational calculator as absurd. The general principle of incarnation with a little letter "i" — the idea that meaning is embodied in the finite, the concrete, the particular — is solemnly consecrated in a way that draws on the metacosmic efficacy of divine transcendence thanks to *the* Incarnation with a big letter "I," when the Word becomes present to the world order in his own Person, in flesh and blood, and therefore space and time. In *The Porch of the Second Virtue*, Péguy remarks:

> All our days, you will say, are the same on earth,
> setting out from the same mornings they carry us on the
> road to the same evenings.[75]

Ah, but they never lead you to the same eternal evenings.

Christoph Schönborn, the cardinal-archbishop of Vienna, has written:

> As Old Testament prophecy proceeds, the coming of God is described ever more clearly as a coming which will "make all things new" (cf. Isaiah 43,19). . . . Here Christ's conception acquires its full range of application: here is the man whose existence is entirely new, right from the roots. In the midst of a world where anything new simply replaces something old, only to become old in its turn, there is now a *new* humanity, a human life which does not at its conception have the germ of death in it, but comes forth entirely out of God's newness.[76]

If we want to see what it is like for the grace of the Son of man to reinvigorate the earth, we must look with Péguy to the saints who have now taken the place once enjoyed under the Old Covenant by the prophets. They are the ones who renew human life by divine life, finding the source of this renewal in their union with Christ. *Prima facie*, the results will not always be spectacular, but the causality of grace often works by underground streams.[77]

True, orientation to the supernatural has to begin from the acceptance of nature, but that is because, in Chesterton's words, nature is always seeking the supernatural, not because they are essentially the same.

Typical of misunderstandings in this realm is that they drain the drama from the scheme of salvation. The reason why the Incarnation begins with a birth is not to settle us in a humanistic complacency. Instead, the Incarnation begins with a birth to draw our attention to the fact that we, like the whole earth, now *have*

a chance. To be born is to have a chance on the level of nature —
that is why, indeed, childbirth *is* already good, beautiful, and
blessed, as well as pathetic and worrying. Analogously, the Incarnation is a chance of salvation given to man. To presume on salvation — to take it for granted that everyone will "get to the
boat" eventually, to canonize the dead instantaneously in the fashion so common now in Catholic funeral practice — is to miss
the way the divine plan of salvation revealed in the "Fleshtaking"
echoes the fragile beauty and dramatic adventure of human life
itself.

Recovered innocence and the unfading freshness of grace can
only be experienced by those who respond to a divinely enabled
new beginning — even if, in each human birth, there is disclosed
something of the miracle shown in the birth at Bethlehem: the
active presence of the eternally youthful Creator in whose saving
power — for Christendom but even more for man — Péguy
placed his hope.

FIVE

༄ᕽᕽ

Martyr of Israel
Edith Stein and the Love of Wisdom

Introduction

Edith Stein entered the world in the Silesian city of Breslau (now Wroclaw, in Poland), in 1891, born into a devout Jewish household — or at any rate, after her father's early death, a household where the *women* were devout. The combination of the words "Silesian" and "Jewish," when juxtaposed with the date, should alert us. If this child should survive to middle age, her path in Hitler's Germany was unlikely to be straight.

Her fragmentary autobiography (but it is a sizable fragment — some four hundred pages in the English translation)[78] was written to furnish Gentile friends with some inkling of what it was like to grow up in a Jewish family. Inevitably, in the charged and ominous circumstances of the early 1930s, it also sought to provide an apologia for her fellow "non-Arians." Rhetorically, she asked:

> Is Judaism represented only by, or even, only genuinely by, powerful capitalists, insolent literati, or those restless heads who have led the revolutionary movements of the past decades?[79]

Owing, perhaps, to this apologetic intent, the chief impression the autobiography gives of her family — her mother's powerful Jewish faith notwithstanding — is its patriotism, founded on a thoroughgoing insertion into German literary culture.

Most of that culture, however, was derived from the sleepy Germany of the old princely states rather than the newly united — and increasingly nationalistic — Germany over which Wilhelm II presided as kaiser. Politics was relevant here because the claim that the Jews had no real sense of identification with civil society was what had sparked the rise of political anti-Semitism in Germany and Austria.

Though Edith Stein's manuscript stops abruptly in the third year of the First World War, her writing technique enabled her to look ahead at various junctures. In a telling scene, she describes how, after the defeat of the Central Powers and the granting by the Allies of independence to Poland, her mother's family corralled their relatives into returning home for the plebiscite in the disputed territory where their native town of Lublinitz was located. When, as a consequence of counting the vote of not only the municipality but also its hinterland, Lublinitz was duly awarded to the Poles, they left in disgust.[80] Such deeply felt Germanness, however, would prove in the event of no avail.

Her mother's energy (she did a man's work, running a lumberyard) guaranteed Edith not only a financially secure upbringing but an excellent education as well. From a very early age, Edith showed an extraordinary aptitude for her schoolbooks. But as the human quality of her memoirs of the family demonstrates, this was not *mere* cleverness. (However, the episode where Edith's sisters dissuade her from reading Schopenhauer's two-volume *The World as Will and Representation* at the age of fifteen suggests that at least some of her siblings were more liberally endowed than she with common sense!)

Her teachers admired her, but their admiration fortunately failed to turn her head. Willing to help with set tasks, she remained popular with her more averagely intelligent fellow-pupils. Lengthy hikes with family and friends in the Riesengebirge, the high mountains separating Silesia from Bohemia, kept her feet on the ground, even if the ground in question was Alpine.

The Philosopher

Edith's introduction to university life was in her home city. In 1811, Frederick William III, king of Prussia, had founded the University of Breslau by the simple device of combining the (largely post-Reformation) University of Frankfurt-an-der-Oder with a local Jesuit College founded in the spirit of the Counter-Reformation by those erstwhile rulers of Silesia, the Habsburgs.

From the beginning, Edith's favorite subject among the humanities was philosophy. Dissatisfied with the teaching she was receiving at Breslau on the psychology of thought, she devoured a copy she had been given of the newly minted *Logical Investigations* of Edmund Husserl, founder of the philosophical school called "phenomenology." She was even more charmed when told by her professor that at Husserl's university, Göttingen, "that's all you do: philosophize, day and night, at meals, in the street, everywhere. All you talk about is 'phenomena.' "[81]

When, accordingly, Edith transferred to the ancient Saxon university town, this socially confident young woman partied — decorously — and with male and female colleagues explored the "carefully husbanded fields, neat villages and . . . encircling wreath of green forests" of what she acclaimed as the "heart of Germany."[82] But above all, she did what she came for. She became the student and subsequently, on his move to Freiburg and the conferring of her own doctorate, the personal academic assistant of Edmund Husserl.

True, the "philosophy of sympathy" of another early phenomenologist, the Catholic convert Max Scheler, was important to her (it provided her with the topic of her doctoral dissertation[83]). But her lifework would be to draw from Husserl's philosophy a way back for European thought to the fountain of metaphysical inspiration that is Aquinas[84] — and to take from Husserl's approach a method that could set out the spiritual experience of Catholic Christianity in a fresh and, as she hoped, newly penetrating guise.[85]

Before outlining her own contribution to Catholic wisdom, something must evidently be said about how a Jew — who, by her own confession, had lost her faith in her schooldays — came to be a member of the Catholic Church. Though she never set out to describe her conversion as such, she certainly reflected on the topic, and the fruits of that reflection can be seen in a number of her posthumously published writings, most especially — in what concerns the heart of the conversion experience — her essay on "The Ontic Structure of the Person," in Volume VI of the *Werke*. That is where she tells how the soul can only find itself and its peace in *das Reich der Gnade*, "the Kingdom of grace."[86] Letters to friends as well as facts about her life story that have long been in the public domain all help to make it possible for a present-day author like the French lay theologian Florent Gaboriau to write a book titled *The Conversion of Edith Stein*.[87]

Edith's most penetrating biographer, the Dutch Carmelite Father Romaeus Leuven, pictures her conversion by drawing together various threads into a tapestry.[88] Her mother's zeal for the Torah, and for prayer, and her conviction that the greatest blessings come as spiritual gifts continued to influence Edith long after she declared herself an unbeliever — but by itself, of course, the example of Jewish piety would not have steered her craft toward Rome.

Edith herself mentions the witness of unselfconscious prayer she was able to observe in Catholic villages and churches in the neighborhood of Göttingen. Then there were Scheler's lectures, and his refusal to exclude the world opened to the eyes of faith from the purview of phenomenology. Then again, there was the conversion to Evangelical Christianity of Adolf Reinach, her predecessor as Husserl's assistant: a conversion she only knew of — but how powerfully! — when in 1917 helping his young widow put his papers in order after his untimely death in the First World War. "This," she would tell her prioress at the Carmel of Echt, "was my first meeting with the Cross and the divine power it gives those who carry it."[89] For five years, she mulled over these experiences and matured a response to them. In her own words:

> In the foundational act of religion, knowledge, love and deed are united.[90]

What enabled Edith to finally make this act, and so seek out the waters of Baptism, was the discovery of a book hitherto unknown to her. The year was 1922, and she was a houseguest in the home of a friend. From the shelf, by "chance," she picked up the book *Life of Teresa of Jesus, by Herself*. Reading right through the night, she finally closed it with the words, "This is the truth"; she meant that — to condense her own (oblique) account — if Teresa is real, then God is real. As she put it later, she could find no more persuasive witness to the realities of which the Catholic religion spoke than the saint of Ávila. Teresa managed it

> through the richness of inner experience this saintly writer had at her disposal, since she had reached the highest step of the mystical life of grace; through her far-from-ordinary capacity for giving an intelligible account of the processes of her inner life, so putting the unsayable into words as to

make it virtually plain and tangible and giving it the stamp of authenticity; through her power of shaping a finished work of art from out of individual actions . . . in their inner coherence.[91]

The next morning, Edith went into town, bought a copy of the Catholic catechism and a missal, studied them, attended Mass, and sought out a priest. Startling him by her peremptory request for Baptism, she was told that Baptism presupposes prior instruction. "Test me," she replied. The rest of her life would do just that.

I have called Edith Stein a "martyr of Israel," and we must come eventually to her death as, specifically, a Jewish Catholic. But I have also identified her with the "love of wisdom," and for this we must gain a fuller grasp of her distinctive approach to the Gospel, which united philosophy with supernatural faith. The most enjoyable way to do so is probably the dialogue she wrote for a (preternatural) encounter of Husserl with St. Thomas Aquinas.

It is late in the evening, too late for normal callers. Husserl is just settling down for a little peace and quiet after a hard day's work when a knock on his study door attracts his attention. Enter a Religious in a black-and-white habit. Husserl has had several members of religious orders in his classes but does not remember seeing this particular costume before. No, says Thomas, but he has heard about Husserl — from a distance. Husserl is happy to have a philosophic chat with a senior, if unknown, colleague, and Aquinas settles down on Husserl's old leather settee.

Thomas congratulates the professor on restoring in phenomenology a really scientific philosophy, after all the "beautiful spirit talk" and "high-flying enthusiasm" that once passed for philosophy in German-speaking Europe. Like Thomas, Husserl thinks that things are inherently intelligible, and that the mind can know their intrinsic "ideas" — even if Thomas would see the perfect, or "absolute," coincidence of mind and "idea" as realized only by God. Husserl may not be aware of the fact, but he has to a degree recovered the "Scholastic inheritance" — despite his regarding Thomism as somewhat naïve in its own "realism." (For Husserl, a clear memory-trace of what it is like to perceive a material object should suffice the philosopher, while Aquinas would rather have him knee-deep in bluebells. For Thomas, immersion in the sensuous reality of things starts off the train of thought that leads to saying *how* they exist as well as *what* they are.)

But, complains Aquinas, something is wrong that is more serious still. Husserl treats knowing as, essentially, an unending progress toward some future, fully comprehensive grasp of phenomena by the human mind. He fails to realize that whereas for natural understanding that may be the best we can do, such understanding is itself "only *one* way":

> Not everything that is inaccessible to [natural understanding] is in every sense inaccessible to our mind in its foundational structure. . . . Full truth *is*. There is a knowing that wholly encompasses it, a knowing that is not infinite process but infinite, peaceable fullness — the divine knowing. . . .

Why should knowing always be prospective, ahead of us, and not primordial, something behind us, and so perhaps a font on which we draw? And indeed, so the Church attests, the divine knowing can communicate itself not simply by way of natural understanding but also through supernatural faith.[92]

And if there is, in that fashion, a way of inhabiting a wider life-world, why should not a phenomenological philosopher — of all people!— be willing to enter there?

At the very least, Scholastics and phenomenologists ought to be able to agree on one thing. What rationalists (the common foe) typically demand is that natural reason establish the limits of reason at large by its own devices. But this is contradictory. While all the time appealing to natural reason alone, rationalism would need to position itself *outside* reason in order to carry out this feat. (Here Edith's Thomas has the humility to admit he never in fact mentioned this excellent argument in his writings.)

So Aquinas affirms what for Husserl is merely an open question: Philosophy can attain its maximum comprehensiveness and its greatest certainty only in union with revealed faith. There is a negative proof of this in what "Thomas" (that is, of course, Edith) identifies in discussion with Husserl as the "egocentric" limitations of phenomenology. Real truth-seekers will surely never rest content with just knowing how the self constructs its own world as things present themselves to consciousness. They will always want to ask that further question: But how and why do things exist?[93] Of course, the unbelieving philosopher

> would not hold as "theses" the truths of faith to which one might have recourse; he would only entertain them as "hypotheses." But to know if the consequences drawn from them correspond to truths of reason or not, there is a common criterion on both sides. With respect to the vision of the whole that permits the believing philosopher to encounter both reason and revelation, the unbeliever should calmly wait to see if he can agree and if he can derive some benefit from a deeper and more ample understanding of being.[94]

Edith held, to her regret, that in his later philosophy Husserl moved away somewhat from ontological realism — which eventually must point to God, the Creator of things. In so doing, he moved some way toward a seeming alternative: "transcendental idealism." In such a philosophy, contrary to what a religiously educated non-specialist might suppose, the "transcendent" is not God. The "transcendent" is only the poor old self as it makes what use it can of the different tools at its disposal for construing the world — inner and outer, the value-free and the value-laden — as it exists for its own consciousness. The concern that originates and unifies Husserl's philosophy, so Thomas (that is, Edith) concludes, is "the transcendentally purified consciousness." By contrast, for Thomas himself (for Edith), it is "God and his relation to creatures."[95] Edith's aim will be, then, a theistic — and indeed, a specifically Christian — phenomenology that presents the world as the world of God, and God not only as Creator but as Redeemer and "Transfigurer" as well. In achieving this aim, she will have to dig down into the deep foundations: to write about "finite and eternal being,"[96] and to consider the (literally) crucial demand the latter makes on the former in the "science of the Cross."[97]

Sister Teresa Benedicta of the Cross

So long as she could pursue a career as a Catholic intellectual, teaching (notably at a college run by Dominican sisters in Speyer, where she undertook a systematic study of Thomas and Thomism, translating for publication the "Disputed Questions on Truth"[98]) and lecturing widely, the priests who counseled Edith opposed her desire to pursue a religious vocation. But in 1933, she found herself permanently out of a job. Under new legislation of the incoming Hitler administration, Jews lost their right to participate in the education of German youth. At once, she contacted her spiritual director, the arch-abbot of Beuron, Dom Raphael Walzer. His "apostolic" argument against her entering a cloister had fallen to the ground. A last visit home failed to convince her mother, but the die was cast.

For one who owed her conversion to Teresa of Ávila, "cloister," notwithstanding her love for Benedictine Beuron, could only mean *Carmel*. On April 15, 1934, she received the Carmelite habit, in the presence of a number of former colleagues and pupils, in the Carmel of Cologne. Henceforth, she would be Sister Teresa Benedicta, names to which she added, according to Carmelite custom, the title of devotion "of the Cross." How pertinent that coda to her name would be.

Edith had early spotted the inevitable direction the Reich government would take if National Socialism came to power. At a time when many Catholics were still willing to give Hitler the benefit of the doubt, she predicted that after the persecution of the Jews would come the persecution of the Church. In the end, it was her embodiment of both of those qualities that settled her own fate.

In the middle 1930s, Jews were not only permitted to leave Germany, but the SS actually encouraged them to do so. However, Edith delayed. Her application to transfer to the Carmel of Bethlehem, made in 1938, was turned down. On the last day of the year, she obtained a permit to cross the Dutch border, finding refuge in the Carmel of Echt. She settled well, learned Dutch readily, and made enormous progress in getting into shape her literary output. In 1940, the year Germany invaded the Netherlands, Edith was given the task of writing her distinctive interpretation of the work of St. John of the Cross, in preparation for the 1942 quadricentennial of the birth of the "mystical doctor." Her assignment was prescient. She would soon need this "science of the Cross."

In October 1941, all Jewish emigration from the Reich and the occupied territories was ended. It was no longer appropriate. Some two or three months earlier, a decision to proceed with the extermination of the Jews had been made. So it was that the German state embarked on a program that rendered some half million of its people complicit in the attempted "final solution" to the Jewish "problem."[99]

Across the frontier, the bishop of Roermond assured the sisters at Echt that Catholic Jews were in no danger. But the pastoral letter of the Dutch bishops of July 11, 1942, protesting the decision to deport other Jews in the Netherlands, aroused the fury of Nazi officials. The refusal of the archbishop of Utrecht, the Dutch primate, to call off the public reading of the letter in churches prompted a speech from the German military commander in The Hague identifying Catholic Jews as the Führer's most dangerous opponents. On August 2, they came for Edith.

With some Jewish Dominicans and Cistercians (all, like Edith, traveling in their habits), she was taken by train to Assen, the stop for the camp of Westerbork. Theirs was one of the first deportations there, so the name told them nothing. Edith was notably silent — perhaps, so one of her companions of those days surmised, she alone was aware there would now be no relief. (The others were chattering about future missionary journeys.[100]) On August 7, just thirteen short of a thousand Jews, Edith among them, were dispatched to Auschwitz. At one of the intervening stations, Schifferstadt, there happened to be on the platform a priest who had known Edith slightly in Speyer when she taught with the Dominican sisters there. A supply train came into the station, and attached to it was a single passenger car with soldiers in it. Hearing sounds in the freight cars, he assumed that the train was carrying livestock. Soon it became apparent that the sounds were human voices. Two eyes appeared at a slit:

"Weren't you in the seminary? I know you!" "I am Sister Benedicta, Edith Stein."[101]

It was the last human act her historical record furnishes. One could hardly call human her gassing on August 9, 1942, under the title "No. 44074."

On October 11, 1998, Pope John Paul II canonized "this eminent daughter of Israel and the faithful daughter of the Church." In his homily, the pope said of her:

She traveled the arduous path of philosophy with passionate enthusiasm. Eventually she was rewarded: she seized the truth. Or better: she was seized by it. Then she discovered that truth had a name: Jesus Christ. . . . The quest for truth and its expression in love did not seem at odds to her; on the contrary she realized that they call for one another.[102]

SIX

Passionate Sage
Charles Williams and the Love of the Human City

Life and Work

Charles Williams, like the present writer, was born an English-man. In many ways, and despite his love of London and "Logres" (that is, Britain in the eye of God), a less typical modern denizen of this island than Williams would be hard to find. But equally hard to find would be a more passionate lover of the corporate community as the icon — potentially, at least — of the City of God. And since all spirituality worth the name has to include the *social* dimension of life together, resisting the temptation to take refuge in mere interiority, Williams — or someone much resembling him — must figure in our list.

> For most of his life [thus wrote the chief authority on this "poet of theology"] Charles Williams was a Londoner. City life was the perennial inspiration of his work; a vision of diversity in unity, of the interconnection of innumerable parts within a living whole. Houses, streets, subways, shops, churches provide the background of his early poetry, while the way in which they functioned was to be the mainspring of his interpretation of literature, history and religion. At the root of everything he wrote is his feeling for community.[103]

Charles Walter Stansby Williams was born in 1886 in Hollo-way, a rather dull part of north London. His father worked as a clerk in the city, had literary tastes, and like his wife, was devout-ly Anglican. City and church were the two "companies" around which Charles Williams's imagination revolved, an imagination nourished by the Bible, orthodox Christian doctrine, English poetry, and people.

When Charles was eight, the family moved, on medical ad-vice to improve his father's health, to the Hertfordshire country town of St. Albans, the erstwhile Roman city of Verulamium, where Williams *père* opened a shop selling artists' materials. Though the elder Williams's health, and notably eyesight, im-proved little, he proved a fine educator of his child. He not only advocated the hearing of all sides to an argument (notably, the fair hearing of objections to Christian believing) and absolute accuracy in matters of fact, but he also exemplified wholehearted commitment to the Christian Gospel. The combination made for an intelligent and durable faith. All his life, Charles hated the refusal to put questions to revelation on the spurious ground that "our little minds were never meant": "Fortunately there is the Book of Job to make it clear that our little minds *were* meant."[104]

His working life as a proofreader and then (as his career progressed) editor for the Oxford University Press — first in its London incarnation at Amen House, near St. Paul's Cathedral, and subsequently, with the coming of the London "Blitz," at Oxford itself — was outwardly ordinary, not to say banal. It concealed the passionate mysticism of a Christian thinker of great depth who was also a director of souls. A varied literary output could not hide a unified sensibility, though his studies of the canon of English poetry, as well as his historical biogra-phies and plays, are of less immediate service for an understanding of his spiritual doctrine than are his theological writings, novels, and later poetry.

Poems, Novels, Theology

The mature *poetry* is, it must be admitted, difficult, because it superimposes Williams's own Christian mythmaking on an already complex cycle of myths and legends — the group that circled around King Arthur, the Romano-British Christian ruler left to face, with the collapse of imperial authority, the barbarian invasions in Late Antique Britain. That group includes those stories found in the medieval Welsh epic, the *Mabinogion,* and, not least, the story of the Grail, the cup used by the Savior at the Last Supper. For Williams's spirituality of "the City," it is, however, indispensable.[105]

The *novels*, described by one critic as "spiritual shockers," explore with sometimes frightening intensity states of soul that are versions of everyday temptations — or gracious possibilities — writ large. The interest they betray in the occult has proved repellent for some Christian — especially perhaps Evangelical – readers. What would Williams have said in his defense?

First, that, like it or not, the practice of magic — whether, to use the Renaissance distinction, *magia* ("white" magic) or *goetia* ("black" magic) — is a human reality that can be encountered in the backstreets or the polite salons of society, and deserves study as such. (That was the spirit in which, at T. S. Eliot's behest, Williams wrote his *Witchcraft* for Faber and Faber.) Secondly, since, as he profoundly believed on general metaphysical as well as Judeo-Christian grounds, this world is a world set within a greater one that provides it with its spiritual infrastructure, there *may* indeed be powers at work — let us call them, broadly, "angelic" — whether for good or evil. (Notice, however, that in his main dogmatic study, *He Came Down from Heaven*, Williams simply leaves open the question of angelic *evil*.) So thirdly, and most importantly, the occult powers and phenomena that occur so regularly in his novels are striking metaphors for aspects of the devices and desires, the spiritual condition and agency, of human hearts.[106] In his study of witchcraft, he wrote wryly:

> No one will derive any knowledge of initiation from this book; if he wishes to meet "the tall, black man" or to find the proper way of using the Reversed Pentegram, he must rely on his own heart, which will, no doubt, be one way or other sufficient.[107]

Finally, the *theological works* are the most germane for our purpose here — and certainly do not lack the imagistic power and sinewy metaphysical underpinnings of the poems and novels.

'The Descent of the Dove'

This is Williams's name not only for perhaps the most successful of his theological studies, but also for the foundation of that "co-inherence" which is the Church or, as he often prefers to write, "Christendom." Williams preferred that venerable name because he saw the Church as not just a religious organization within civil society, but even more as the anticipatory expression on earth of the "whole redeemed City."[108] His New Testament imagination was governed not only by the Incarnation, Baptism, Cross, and Glorification of "Messias" (his customary name for the incarnate Son). It was equally dominated by two Descents: that of "Our Lord the Spirit" at Pentecost and of the New Jerusalem at the End. Consequently, communities, corporate bodies, and cities — and anti-cities like Babel — are often found to dominate his theological thought. "The City" — nearly always capitalized — is more than the Church; or rather, it is the Church when she is gloriously, in all plenitude, herself:

> The Kingdom — or, apocalyptically, the City — is the state into which Christendom is called; but, except in vision, she is not yet the City. The City is the state which the Church is to become.[109]

Not that Williams minimizes the "state" the Church has already reached, thanks to the work of Messias and "Our Lord the Spirit." In the Church, something with universal implications has happened to fallen nature. There has come about "a new state of being, a state of redemption, of co-inherence." This "new state" was made actual by the divine "substitution" that the Redeemer enacted in his Incarnation and Atonement, when he took our nature and bore our sins, and the grace of his humiliation and sacrifice was communicated to us by the Holy Spirit.[110] Williams understands Paul and John very well. By treading in the apostles' footsteps, the writers of the sub-apostolic age were able to overcome the challenge of Gnosticism, with its claim that the true "upper spiritual classes" lived by a knowledge superior to that of mere believers. As Williams explains:

> Faith was not a poor substitute for vision; it was rather the capacity for integrating the whole being with truth. It was a total disposition and a total act. By definition all men were in need of salvation; therefore, of faith and repentance in faith.[111]

Moreover, Williams presents the Church, from the time of the early apologists onward, as making "preparations for drawing into herself the whole of normal human existence."[112] That hope was realized — in principle — in the Constantinian settlement. Unlike many later twentieth-century Christian writers who, certain Liberationists and Neo-traditionalists apart, seem ashamed of the Church's taking spiritual responsibility for civil society, Williams exults in the moment when Constantine accepted the duties of "bishop of the relations of the Church to the world at large" (the phrase comes from Eusebius, the first Church historian), and so became "the crowned point of union between the supernatural and the natural":[113]

> The adorned figure of the Emperor, throned among the thirty score of prelates, hearing and declaring with them the witness of all the churches to the apostolic tradition, signifies many things. There the acceptance of time was completely manifested; there a new basis — a metaphysical basis — was ordained for society. . . . Intellect was accepted, marriage was accepted, ordinary life was accepted. The early vision of St Peter was found to have wider meanings than had been supposed: 'what I have cleansed that call not thou common'. The nature of the Church had not changed, and only fools suppose that it had. It remained reconciliation and sin redeemed.[114]

Williams does not deny, however, that the ascetic reaction of Christian monasticism to a too-settled and civilly powerful Christendom was legitimate. "Fashionable" conversion in the Greco-Roman world — like mass or even forced conversion in the world of the barbarian newcomers — made the Church's victory too easily won:

[This] produced in her children a great tendency to be aware of evil rather than of sin, meaning by evil the wickedness done by others, by sin the wickedness done by oneself.[115]

Practitioners of the "Positive Way" — summed up in the magnificence of the conciliar assembly where bishops surrounded the bejeweled person of the emperor — needed the very different testimony of those who walked the "Negative Way," the monks of the desert:

The one Way was to affirm all things orderly until the universe throbbed with vitality; the other to reject all things until there was nothing anywhere but He. The Way of Affirmation was to develop great art and romantic love and marriage and philosophy and social justice; the Way of Rejection was to break out continually in the profound mystical documents of the soul. . . .[116]

And in any case, the Communion of the Holy Eucharist joined the two — the city-builders and the anchorites — into one. There they met in a holy fellowship of mutual respect, for "images can be as disciplinary as their lack."[117] Toward the end of his life, the great sixteenth-century ascetic and mystic John of the Cross was "encouraged to remember that he liked asparagus; our Lord the Spirit is reluctant to allow either of the two great Ways to flourish without some courtesy to the other."[118]

Not that Williams is starry-eyed in judging the record of those who acted to build the City in the name of the Church. Though heresy refuses the "common fact of supernatural exchange," the attempt to suppress it via capital punishment wielded by emperor or prince went against the Kingdom:

There has never yet been found any method of driving out
one devil — except by pure love — which does not allow
the entrance of seven, as Messias had long ago pointed
out. . . . Deep, deeper than we believe lie the roots of sin; it
is in the good that they exist; it is in the good that they
thrive and send up sap and produce the black fruit of hell.
The peacock fans of holy and austere popes drove the ashes
of burning men over Christendom.[119]

Where a Christendom society fails in its practices to reflect
the co-inherence, the practice of co-inherence is driven back into
the hearts of the saints. But Christendom is never content with
that. (We see as much in Dante, among whose central "images"
for Love are Empire and Church.)

The Nature of the Co-inherence

The pattern for human sociability is set, first of all, by the doctrines of the Trinity and creation; then by those of the Incarnation, the Atonement, and the "substituted surrender of
Himself";[120] and by the sacramental continuation of these, the
Holy Eucharist. These are the "places" where we discover what
the human city means — or, rather, what being called to "co-
inherence" is *meant to mean*.

First, as Trinitarian dogma teaches, "the Godhead itself [is] in
Co-inherence."[121] As Williams presents Origen of Alexandria's teaching on the Sonship of Christ, co-inherence is voluntary union through
obedience and joy. In the very Deity, there is the joy of obedience,
and obedience is the only means of its particular joy. The Son "co-
inheres obediently and filially in the Father, as the Father authorita-
tively and paternally co-inheres in him."[122] To affirm, then, with
Athanasius, against the Arians, the pre-existence of such a Son is to

say that there was never a time when Love (not mere benevolence but *exchange*) was not.

And simply by dint of our creation, a refraction of this co-inherence is seen in us. Birth itself shows as much: What exchange could be more primal than the new life that comes from the transference of seed? Our solidarity with one another, though, goes further than this. In his account of our relation not only to Christ but to Adam, Augustine, says Williams, "was aiming at the same principle of inevitable relationship which . . . governed the orthodoxy of the Church."

> Whatever ages of time lay between us and Adam, yet we were in him and we were him; more, we sinned in him and his guilt is in us. And if indeed mankind is held together by its web of existence, then ages cannot separate one from another. Exchange, substitution, co-inherence are a natural fact as well as a supernatural truth. . . . The co-inherence reaches back to the beginning as it stretches on to the end, and the *anthropos* is present everywhere. . . . [C]o-inherence did not begin with Christianity; all that happened was that co-inherence itself was redeemed and revealed by that very redemption as a supernatural principle as well as a natural.[123]

The covenant with Noah, with its warning — "At the hand of every man, and of his brother, will I require the life of man" (Genesis 9, 5b; Douay Version) — points to the human creation as co-inherence in becoming:

> It is a declaration of an exchange of responsibility rather than of joy, but the web of substitution is to that extent

created, however distant from the high end and utter conclusion of entire interchange.[124]

Secondly, then, the source of the *full* co-inherence idea must
be sought in the specifically Christological doctrines of Incarnation, Atonement, and Eucharist. The birth and sacrifice of the
Word Incarnate restore the Trinitarian pattern that the human
creation was meant to show:

> By an act of substitution he reconciled the natural world
> with the world of the kingdom of heaven, sensuality with
> substance. He restored substitution and co-inherence ev-
> erywhere; up and down the ladder of that great substitu-
> tion all our lesser substitutions run; within that sublime
> co-inherence all our lesser co-inherences inhere.[125]

The role of the godparents at infant Baptism shows it mark-
ing Christian initiation from the first:

> The method of the new life which Messias (he said) came
> to give so abundantly begins with substitution and pro-
> ceeds by substitution. . . . All goodness is from that source,
> changed and exchanged in its process. . . . We shall be graced
> by one and by all, only never by ourselves. . . .[126]

This is supremely shown in the Mass. For Williams, the high
point of its expression is the declaration "On the Catholic Faith,"
which, at Innocent III's request, prefaced the decrees of the Fourth
Lateran Council. In the Eucharist, in the council's words, "to
effect the mystery of unity, we ourselves receive of that which is
his what he himself received of that which is ours" — a statement

that Williams calls a "lyric of theology," in which "the doctrine of exchange, of substitution, of co-inherence reached its highest objective point on earth."[127]

After Pentecost, by a gradual process, the "great doctrines of interchange, of the City" are uncovered. We find them presupposed in the saying ascribed to the ascetic Anthony of Egypt, "Your life and your death are with your neighbor," and in the explanation given by the Carthaginian martyr Felicitas to her jailers, "[Tomorrow] another will be in me who will suffer for me." And, in any case, it is all precontained in the words of the Christ of St. John's Gospel: "they in me and I in them."[128] Augustine showed how, through predestining grace,

> the City of God leaps upon its citizens, presiding like the god Vaticanus over the first wail of the child, separating it for ever from the transient earthly cities, making it a pilgrim and a sojourner.[129]

The Human City

It is clear that, for Williams, the city has many dimensions. It cannot be thought without the Church, nor without the wider cosmos, natural and supernatural, in which it is set. So much emerges from Williams's extraordinary reworking of the Arthurian cycle in the Taliessin poems. It would be foolish to translate the symbolism of the poems into straightforward politological discourse. In the preface to *The Region of the Summa Stars*, Williams himself tells us that the reader should understand the "Emperor" as "operative Providence." But it would equally be crass to ignore the fact that the subject of the poetry is "the Matter of Britain" — the spiritual origin and destiny of a civil society — while the sequence is permeated by a wider vision of Christendom. In *The Descent of the Dove*,

Williams makes plain his *beau idéal* of historic Christendom: the emperor in Byzantium, the pope in Rome. What interests Williams is not the historical contingency of the location of the imperial city on the Bosporus. What interests him is, rather, the "living form" of the emperor considered as

> the single figure in which were exhibited the two complementary offices of men, sacred and secular, as the two Natures had been united in Christ.

When, in 1453, the city fell to the Ottoman forces, government, in passing to the caliph of Islam, passed to one who

> expressed in his own person the separation of the two Natures as the Emperor expressed their union.[130]

What, then, of the pope in Rome? As an Anglo-Catholic with some leanings toward Rome and as a young man in St. Albans, he had belonged to a discussion group, the "Theological Smokers," who

> over pipes, cigarettes, coffee and cakes explored the universe, regretted nonconformity, had a sneaking regard for but kept a wary eye on His Holiness. . . .[131]

Williams had no intention of undermining the "supernatural hypothesis of the Apostolic See,"[132] even though he could see the natural factors that had favored Rome's rise to ecclesial primacy. In *The Region of the Summer Stars*, as the Christian empire disintegrates under the barbarian onslaught and the centrifugal forces of what in our nature remains unredeemed, the role of the pope in sustaining the unity of the City comes into its own. At Mass, in the Lateran Basilica, Pope Deodatus becomes, by his offering of the Holy Sacrifice, a conduit for supernatural communion and rekindles hope for the City's future, the future of humankind in its relation to God:

> The Pope passed to sing the Christmas Eucharist.
> He invoked peace on the bodies and souls of the dead,
> yoked fast to him and he to them,
> co-inherent all in Adam and all in Christ. . . .
> The gnosis of separation in the Pope's soul
> had become a promulgation of sacred union,
> and he his function only; at the junction of communion
> he offered his soul's health for the living corpses,
> his guilt, his richness of repentance, wealth for woe.
> This was the Pope's prayer; prayer is substance;
> quick the crowd, the thick souls of the dead,
> moved in the Pope's substance to the invoked Body,
> the Body of the Eucharist, the Body of the total loss,
> the unimaged loss; the Body salvaged the bodies
> in the fair, sweet strength of the Pope's prayer.
> The easement of exchange led into Christ's appeasement
> under the heart-breaking manual acts of the Pope.
> . . . consuls and lords within the Empire
> . . . felt the Empire
> revive in a live hope of the Sacred City.[133]

It is apparent that, for Williams, you cannot serve the human city unless you serve the ecclesial — and vice versa. There can be no merely natural philanthropy, no service of others that is merely humane, no attention to the good of the temporal that ignores the spiritual, just as, conversely, work for the Church, if it is truly ordered to the City of God, will be open to all sorts and conditions of men in their various needs. This is a fruitful ambiguity since "the other world co-inhere[s] in this and this co-inhere[s] in the other."[134]

Still, the point of the City is ultimately a simple one. It is to reverse the anti-community of the Fall. The story of Cain and Abel, following hard on the heels of the "knowing of good and evil" by "the Adam" (Williams's corporate singular for Adam and Eve) gives us a grim lesson:

> Human relationship has become to a man a source of anger and hate, and the hatred in its turn brings more desolation.[135]

The human desire to know the good as something other than good, to introduce into the good a contradiction of itself, spelt ruin for the city of man. Failure in the "communion of justice" spoils "all the relations between the I AM and the people," even though the communion of justice is "not sufficient in itself; it is to be perfected by adoration."[136] Williams is fierce when addressing modern Christendom's failing the poor. Neediness can only be used as "the Way" by those advanced in holiness. No such "terrible Rejection of Images" can be imposed upon the "co-inheritors of glory."[137] As a dreadful warning, atheistic Communism was allowed to establish its own "co-inherence," but it could not redeem the past. "That co-inherence could not reach the millions who had died in their misery; the Republic of the future was to be raised on their bones."[138] That is not the true City, which is all-inclusive, save for those who choose perpetual exile.

Charles Williams does not spell out any preferred political form for the civil embodiment of the City, much less any political program. His agenda was this: bearing one another's burdens, a discipline he saw, one conjectures, as more demanding than occasional visits to a polling booth. He was keen to divest the notion of bearing one another's burdens of any suggestion that it basically consisted in being sympathetic, and saying, Snoopy-like, to those in need, "Be of good cheer." In *Descent into Hell,* the wise Peter Wentworth tells Pauline Anstruther (of whom a great act of substituted love will be asked) that, while listening sympathetically no doubt helps, what the New Testament means by the bearing of others' burdens is far closer to carrying someone else's parcel: "To bear a burden is precisely to carry it instead of."[139] And in his wartime essay "The Redeemed City," he wrote:

> More, much more, might be done by the practice of it between ourselves by intellectual and spiritual methods. Mental burdens can be carried as well as physical; and even physical more than we know. The very healing of the flesh might be hastened by it. It is not the reward of sanctity; it is a way of sanctity, but also it is the only way of bearable life.[140]

He looked to the "transfiguration of the earthly State into the heavenly City" — whose "alteration" he saw as the work of the Holy Spirit in the Church, insisting, moreover, that it "is an age-long work," which, even when "general work . . . must be done individually."[141] To grasp what he meant by this change in the ethos of the human city means getting hold of his entire account of substituted love in the co-inherence. He dreamed that in a "profoundly Christian State" the Church might found a guild of those who would vicariously bear the legal penalties laid on criminals. If we say that surely *is* a dream, Williams replies:

> Only by operations that once seemed no less of dreams has the Church reached its own present self-consciousness — by devotions not dissimilar, powers not otherwise practised.[142]

SEVEN

Theological Artist
Leonid Ouspensky and the Love of Sacred Beauty

Image and Icon

Asceticism entails avoiding harmful images, and spirituality entails seeking out healthful ones: images that heal and elevate the sinful mind, heart, and passions through their evangelical beauty. The images of Christendom's sacred art are eye baths for the soul. Such images do not all have to be icons, in the strict sense of panel images of holy figures as seen in the Byzantine tradition. But even a Western Catholic may surely concede that the art of the Byzantine-Slav icon exemplifies to a unique degree what should be the case about all Christian art in whatever style, all the Church's "iconography."[143]

In point of fact, an iconic art scarcely if at all distinguishable from that of the Byzantine East was known in the Latin West in the patristic and medieval periods. Indeed, one historian of the image has written that

> Rome in late antiquity and the early Middle Ages must be
> considered a Byzantine province as regards the veneration
> of icons. This is significant insofar as Rome was the center
> of Western Christendom. . . . In Rome the icon had an older
> and more untroubled existence than even in Byzantium.[144]

The papacy, after all, was never troubled by Iconoclasm in the way that the Byzantine patriarchate had to suffer.

Moreover, if we define icons (as we should) as painterly presentations of holy persons or holy mysteries key to the faith in some kind of cultic context, we can say that certain historic images of this type were still considered to be special vehicles of grace, and continued to serve as foci of devotion in Western Catholicism, well beyond the medieval epoch. The German language has good names for them: *Andachtsbilder*, images for loving meditation, or *Gnadenbilder*, images of (that is, mediations of) grace.

An Unusual Background

It is not, however, to the interpreters of such Latin icons that I shall turn, but rather to an outstanding twentieth-century Eastern Orthodox commentator on the art of the icon, who was himself a renowned icon-painter in the Russian tradition. Leonid Ouspensky can provide us with a point of entry to all that the spiritual beauty of the icon can offer us by way of rejuvenation of our Christian lives.

Ouspensky's early life story is the tale of an extraordinary *volte-face*. He was one of those people who, with a fitting humility about past errors, came to adore what he had burned: in his case, the Holy Face of Christ, as it appeared in the art of the icon, surrounded by the images of the Blessed Mother and the saints.

Ouspensky was born in the pre-revolutionary Russian countryside. His father was a member of the minor provincial nobility, and his mother was from the peasant class. When he was twelve, the First World War broke out. At first, there was little disruption to his home life — except that when the farm laborers were mobilized, he and his father had to help with the scything in their own fields, an activity he greatly enjoyed. But in 1917, the

October Revolution soon reached the town where Ouspensky did his schooling, Zadonsk, famous for its saintly bishop Tikhon (1724-1783), who had been canonized some fifty years earlier.

Turbulent, momentous times can make children prematurely adult. The fifteen-year-old Ouspensky, fired by revolutionary zeal, took a lead in the Sovietizing of his school and the general life of the neighborhood. Declaring himself a convinced atheist, he toured the local villages, haranguing the inhabitants for their subservience to the Church. He took particular delight in invading their houses in order to seize the icons, which were a feature of every devout Russian home, chucking them unceremoniously out of cottage windows. In later years, when he came to study the theology and history of the icon, he would discover how in fifteenth-century Novgorod, and later Moscow, adherents of a rationalistic return to the Old Testament had been his predecessors in depositing icons into dustbins.[145]

In 1918, Ouspensky joined the Red Army. Since peace had been made with the Central Powers at the Treaty of Brest Litovsk, the task of that army was the pulverization of its monarchist and other opponents, by means of the Russian Civil War.

Ouspensky's military life lasted for barely two years. In the summer of 1920, while his cavalry division was focused on subduing the hardy inhabitants of the Caucasus, who were resisting Bolshevism, his troop was surrounded by White artillery. His horse shot from beneath him, Ouspensky was taken prisoner and condemned to summary execution — from which fate, however, a passing colonel of the White Army saved him.

The months he spent as a captive under surveillance, when a false word could have spelled death, made him into a man of few words for the rest of his life. In a setting with nothing human to commend it, he noticed for the first time, according to his widow,

Lydia, the beauty of grass.[146] Perhaps in response to that humble creation, there awakened in him the love of beauty — and above all, the beauty of God — which would take him through Parisian art school to a life of painstaking devotion to the sacred art of the Church.

Rediscovering the Icon

Meanwhile, however, there were hard, joyless times. Evacuated with the defeated White Army from the Crimea, he was eventually released in Bulgaria, malnourished (he went blind for a while), and able to find only crushing manual work as a coal miner. How, then, did he reach France, his eventual home?

Owing to the bloodletting of the First World War, French industry was desperate for workers, and industrialists' agents scoured Eastern Europe in search of labor. It was as a worker in a bicycle factory and, subsequently, a part-time unloader of freight trains that he enrolled in the school of painting founded by a Russian émigré, Tatiana Soukhotina, Tolstoy's daughter.

Ouspensky painted his first icon on a bet, but the experience staggered him. "It was by means of the icon that he came back to the faith and the Church."[147] He took a few lessons from an established iconographer, but Ouspensky's money ran out. Instead, he studied the numerous icons, once owned by refugees, that could be found in Parisian antique shops. They were, he maintained, his real professors. He found support in an Orthodox confraternity, the Confrérie Saint-Photius-le Confesseur, which provided intellectual leadership for those Russian Orthodox who, unlike many in Paris, still adhered to the Moscow patriarchate despite the latter's collusion with the Soviet authorities.[148] (Here I must mention the name of the great dogmatic theologian Vladimir Lossky.)

During the Second World War, Ouspensky was mobilized by the German authorities in the occupied zone for industrial war work, escaped, lived clandestinely in Paris, and during the liberation was again (owing to a misunderstanding) almost shot. Despite everything, it was a period of great productivity in his output of icons. And after the war ended, the Confrérie established an Institut Saint-Denis, where Ouspensky taught iconology (the theology of icons) and iconography (the technique of their making): The material from these courses would contribute to the making of his books on the icon, which have been influential, especially in Orthodox countries.

Ouspensky was an indefatigable worker. He spent thirteen or fourteen hours of the day on painting, restoring, woodcarving, stone sculpting and metalwork; evenings and feast days were for his writing. He was shy of public speaking. He died on December 12, 1987, and was buried in the Russian graveyard at Sainte-Geneviève-des-Bois.

Understanding the Art of the Icon

What was Ouspensky's understanding of the art of the icon, of its importance for the spiritual life of the Church and, hence, for the spirituality of her members? Christianity, so Ouspensky argues, is the revelation of the God-Man not only as the Word sent from the Father but also as the Image of God. In the Byzantine rite, there is a feast of the Holy Face of the Savior — and a devotion expressed in similar terms was well known in the Western Middle Ages: Ouspensky makes much of the liturgical texts that spell out the meaning of this celebration.[149]

In the early Syrian Church, there is a tradition to the effect that the Savior permitted a portrait to be painted of him in his lifetime: the famous "Mandylion" of Edessa.[150] Similarly, in Greek and Latin Christianity, there is the claim that the mother of Jesus was the subject of a painting by the evangelist Luke. The Mandylion disappeared in the chaos of the Fourth Crusade, and Ouspensky admits that those icons of the Mother and Child that bear the name "Lucan" can only be copies of copies. But he sees these historic claims as testifying to a more foundational conviction in the Church: namely, that

> right from the beginning there had been a clear understand-
> ing of the significance and possibilities of the image, and
> that the attitude of the Church towards it never changed,
> since it is derived from the actual teaching on the Divine
> Incarnation.[151]

The same is true, evidently, of claims that certain images of the Word Incarnate came into being miraculously: images "not made by hands," of which the earliest and best known in Byzantine Christianity was the fourth-century "Camuliana" (so called from the village in what is now Turkey, where it was found), a copy of which, in all likelihood, was the image of Christ brought by Augustine to Canterbury in 597.[152] The Western equivalent of such miraculous images would be the "Vernicle," the outline of the Lord's face imprinted on the cloth with which one of the Jerusalem women wiped his brow on the Way of the Cross.[153] (The Shroud of Turin belongs here likewise.)

Whatever one makes of the claim that divine power was causally at work in the making of these images, it is easy to see that at the level of symbolism they offer a striking testimony to the basic Christian affirmation. The divine Father, by his own free initiative in love and mercy, has given to the world his own perfect image, Jesus Christ. The iconic, we can say, has always existed since the time of the apostles — indeed, since the time of Christ himself, in the sense that with the Incarnation the divine makes itself known by means of the visual order, when the Word takes flesh. The actual production of Christian artworks follows ineluctably from this.

A Little History of Our Subject

Leaving aside the dimension of miracle, Ouspensky sees nothing improbable in the notion of early Christian portraiture, since the art of portrait painting was flourishing in the Greco-Roman world, even as the Gospel moved out into the Gentile context. He is impressed by the report of the first Church historian, Eusebius of Caesarea, that, although personally he disapproved of such images (Eusebius's theology is weak on the significance of the Word's entering the *incarnate* order), he did not deny their existence. Ouspensky recognizes that the material culture of the Church underwent development; gradually, by sifting out incongruous elements in the different artistic styles of antiquity, she shaped a form of sacred art well suited to the Gospel proclamation. But he also strongly emphasizes the speed and sureness with which this process of discernment took place.

Thus, as early as the Roman catacombs, basic principles are in place:

> The fundamental principle of this art is a pictorial expression of the teaching of the Church, by representing concrete events of sacred History and indicating their inner meaning. . . . The image is reduced to a minimum of detail and a maximum of expressiveness. The great majority of figures are represented with their faces turned towards the congregation, for the importance lies not only in the action

and interaction of the persons represented, but also in their
state, which is usually a state of prayer. . . . [The artist]
cleansed his work of everything personal and remained anon-
ymous; his essential concern was to transmit tradition.[154]

Then, in the first three centuries of the Christianized empire,
after Constantine, further steps are taken. First, the use of symbols
— some of them, like the Orpheus figure or the philosophic Shepherd, shared with Greco-Roman paganism — gives way to a more
fully representational art, frequently monumental in scale and comprehensive in scope, as with the biblical scenes in mosaic that dec-
orate the early Christian basilicas of Ravenna. Ouspensky
emphasizes the very secondary function played by even Old Testament symbols of Christ, "types and foreshadowings," after the
"Quinisext Council" of 692, which decreed that, in the future,
what must above all be depicted is the human form of the Word in
his "life in the flesh, his suffering and his saving death and the
deliverance that issued from it for the world."[155] (Later in his story,
though, he will have to find a place for the popular Russian iconographic motif of the "Old Testament Trinity," a symbolic exegesis
of the three strangers or angels who supped with Abraham at the
Oak of Mamre in the Book of Genesis.)
  Secondly, at a time when the festal cycle of the Church's Liturgy was becoming fixed, iconographic schemes were worked out
for its accompaniment. One of the wonderful oil vases ("ampul-
lae") found at Monza in northern Italy — and dating from some
time between the fourth and sixth centuries — carries no fewer
than seven representations of Gospel episodes closely bound up
with the feasts of the Church: the Annunciation, the Visitation,
the Nativity, the Baptism of Christ, the Crucifixion, the Resur-

rection (in the shape of the myrrh-bearing women going to the tomb), and the Ascension.

Thirdly, Ouspensky suggests that such Fathers of the Church as St. Basil, St. Paulinus, and St. Gregory of Nyssa, under the influence of the ascetic movement, began to appeal to the power of iconography to shape Christian experience and transform Christian behavior. As we shall see, this will be central to Ouspensky's own spiritual theology of the icon, justifying his presence in this book.

Lastly, the Church realizes the confessional value of art, how it can serve to express dogmatic truths. The Council of Ephesus solemnly defines Mary's divine motherhood; images show her as the enthroned Mother, her Son on her knee, angels in attendance, as in the early eighth-century "Madonna of Clemency" in Santa Maria in Trastevere, in Rome.[156] Hence, it was an art truly at the service of the Church's mission that was called into question in the Byzantine Church by the Iconoclasts of the eighth and ninth centuries, but then vindicated by the Iconophile doctors, and notably by two pairs of them: St. Germanus and St. John Damascene, when the crisis opened, and St. Nicephorus and St. Theodore as it closed. Despite his dislike of the later Western Catholic "innovations" in Church art, Ouspensky does full justice to the consistent support Iconophile patriarchs and theologians enjoyed from the Roman popes.

The icons emerged from their baptism of fire with their place in the Church enhanced. The dogmatic definition of the Second Council of Nicaea, in 787, by speaking of Scriptures and images as mutually "indicating" or "explaining" each other, allows Ouspensky to offer his high doctrine of icons, a view common among the twentieth-century Eastern Orthodox:

In the eyes of the Church, the icon is not, then, an art illustrative of Sacred Scripture; it is a language that corresponds to Scripture, that is equivalent to it, corresponding not to the letter of Scripture, nor to the book [the Bible] as an object, but to the Gospel preaching, which means to Scripture's very content, to its meaning, just as the texts of the Liturgy do. That is why the icon plays in the Church the same role as Scripture, it has the same significance: liturgical, dogmatic, educational.[157]

The Icon and the Work of Salvation

Ouspensky underlines the task given the icons in the spiritual lives of believers as he unfolds the implications of this bold statement. The icon yields up the content of Scripture, not in a theoretical way, as some particularly excellent textbook of dogmatic theology might do, but after the fashion of the Church's worship — namely, "in a living way, addressing itself to all the human faculties." It transmits the truth of Scripture "in the light of the whole spiritual experience of the Church, of her Tradition." Icon and Liturgy, the liturgical image and the liturgical word, reinforce each other in such a way that, by their joint means, "Scripture lives in the Church and in each of her members."[158]

What should holy images mean to a Christian disciple? Ouspensky draws on Byzantine liturgical texts, from the Sunday known as the "Triumph of Orthodoxy," to tell us. This is not a bad choice, for the heart of that celebration is rejoicing at the restoration of the icons to the churches and homes of the faithful:

The indescribable Word of the Father has made himself describable by becoming incarnate from you, Mother of God; having re-established the soiled image in its pristine dignity, he unites it to the divine beauty. Confessing salvation, we image it by action and word.

As this "kontakion" (short hymn) makes clear, it is the "kenosis" — that is, the "emptying" of self — of the second divine Person that furnishes the icon with its Christological foundation. We make and venerate icons only because the Person of the Word "emptied himself" by assuming the limitations of a mortal creature (such as humans are), all the while continuing to be and to act in his divine nature, as God almighty. Thanks to his holy Mother, there is Jesus, the God-Man, the *incarnate* Word in his two natures and yet a single Person. Ouspensky emphasizes how, in the art of the Byzantine-Slav icon, even at the Crucifixion, the deepest moment of humiliation in his career, Jesus is never depicted simply as man. (In this sense, the bare crucifix favored by some post-medieval art in the West would be better suited to a Nestorian Christology, where Jesus is a human person.) Rather, he is always shown "theandrically" as the God-Man, in his hidden, yet never-abandoned glory.

The divine Father cannot in himself be represented (Ouspensky touches here on a point furiously debated by Russian churchmen from the sixteenth to the twentieth centuries). The point of the Incarnation is to allow the Father to be shown forth in the Person of the Son when the latter takes on, through Mary, the humanity that renders him depictable in art. By accepting for the Father an iconography independent of the Son's (usually based on the prophetic vision of the "Ancient of Days" in the Book of Daniel), artists and patrons — including patriarchs! — have failed to grasp the fundamental doctrinal claim of the "Council of the Icons," Nicaea II (the seventh ecumenical council), in the year 787.

Unwittingly, those who make or venerate icons of the type called in the East "The Paternity" or the "Synthronon" (in the West, the corresponding image is the late medieval "Throne of Grace") have sidelined Mary as Mother of God, for these representations portray the Trinitarian Persons but not the Mother of the Child. It ceases to be plain why, in the Byzantine kontakion in praise of the restoration of icons, the Church should be addressing herself specifically to the Virgin and to no other.[159]

The Icon and Divine Beauty

The piece of liturgical poetry Ouspensky is discussing goes on to speak of the saving work the Word Incarnate carried out through his life on earth. The Son recreates in humanity the divine image that had been obscured by sin, not only restoring it to the integrity it once enjoyed in Adam but, more than this, giving it a fulfillment Adamic humanity never knew. This further dimension of the saving work of the Word is the gift of everlasting life, which for Ouspensky "consists in the possibility of having access to the divine beauty, the divine glory."[160]

The baptismal life, as expressed in the flourishing of the virtues needed for communion with God, brings this about in us, by the grace of Christ, in the Holy Spirit. Here Ouspensky makes good use of the spiritual maxims of the seventh-century Greek monk Diadochus of Photike:

> In the same way that artists paint in first of all a sketch of the portrait using a single colour, and little by little through the adding of fresh colours increase the likeness of the portrait to its model, . . . so in the same way the grace of God begins in Baptism by remaking the image as it was when man came into existence. Afterward, when it sees us aspir-

ing with all our heart to the beauty of the likeness, . . . add-
ing virtue to virtue, raising up the soul's beauty from glory
to glory, it acquires for the soul the mark of the likeness.[161]

Just as the divine beauty is in Christ before it is in the icon,
so it is in the saint before it is in the saint's image. The "deifica-
tion" (by grace) of Christ's human nature — its plenary sharing
of the Trinitarian life — required the perfect cooperation of Jesus'
human will with his divine will. So likewise, without the commitment of our human freedom in contact with the living God,
baptized Christians cannot be fully renewed in grace and begin
to radiate the divine beauty. From these considerations, based
particularly on St. Paul's second letter to the Church at Corinth,
there arises the special importance in Christology of the mystery
of the Lord's Transfiguration, and also in the history of sanctity
of that high point in nineteenth-century Russian Christian literature, Daniel Motovilov's account (and experience) of the light
surrounding the hermit saint Seraphim of Sarov. Ouspensky himself painted icons of both of these subjects: the Transfiguration
several times, but most notably for the Church of the Three Holy
Hierarchs in the Rue Pétel in Paris; and St. Seraphim, in a much
reproduced icon of which the original belongs to a private collection.[162] "The true beauty," he writes, "is the shining forth of the
Holy Spirit, holiness, participation in the Age to Come." He further explains:

The icon represents not the corruptible flesh that is des-
tined to decomposition, but the transfigured flesh, illumined
by grace, the flesh of the Age to Come. . . . By material
means, visible to carnal eyes, it transmits the divine beauty
and glory. That is why the Fathers call the icon venerable

and holy — because it transmits the deified condition of its prototype and bears his (or her) name. That is why the grace proper to the prototype is found there. In other words, it is the grace of the Holy Spirit that sustains the holiness both of the person represented and of their icon, and it is in that grace that the relation between the Christian and the saint mediated by the icon comes about. The icon shares, so to speak, in the holiness of its prototype and by way of the icon we in our turn share in that holiness in our prayer.[163]

Living Out the Icon in Practice

Finally, we come to the kontakion's practical conclusion. We must confess the salvation attested in the icon, says the text, "by action and word." Confessing it by words is easy enough to understand. Confessing it by actions is slightly more troublesome. Analyzing the "Synodikon" (a liturgical text) of the feast, which anathematizes heretics but proclaims the eternal memory of orthodox confessors, Ouspensky argues that what is in view is a twofold spiritual activity: first and foremost, the "interior labor" of making oneself a "living icon of Christ"; but secondly, the translation of grace into painterly images — visual artworks, as well as the verbal icons of the confessors' truthful words.[164]

The icon, clearly, is more than an aesthetic reality. It expresses the beauty of holiness, which is sharing in the divine life. It reflects the spiritual experience of the saints, from the holy apostles onward, and invites Christians to follow the path of discipleship into the glory of the Kingdom. The use of line and color in the art of the icon is ordered to expressing the effect of uncreated grace on human nature: The icon is incomprehensible without a grasp of Christian asceticism. It is a figural expression of the ascetic discipline that, through grace, can lead all the members of the Church to holiness. It manifests prayer, stimulates prayer, and requires an atmosphere of prayer from would-be iconographers, those who want to use their skills to shape sacred images in line with the tradition of the Church. The icon is a stranger to sentimental (or even unsentimental) naturalism, which simply imitates the unsaved state of things, just as, equally, it is alien to an artistic abstractionism that would ignore the Incarnation, when God took on human form, a human figure.

The Icon and the Cosmic Future

Ouspensky emphasizes, finally, the cosmic aspect of iconography. Here, despite his disdain for iconographic innovation, he refers particularly to certain later types of (especially) Russian icons — those known as "Let every breath praise the Lord" and "In Thee rejoices the whole creation" — that embody this theme: the unity of creation, from beast to angel, around the Savior.

> Harmony and peace re-established, the Church embracing the whole world, this is the central thought of orthodox sacred art, governing architecture as much as painting.[165]

But even in more traditional icons (not those that portray the *sobornost*, or "togetherness," of all creation, but simply, for example, some particular saint), the changed aspect of the environment of the sacred figure (whether this environment be human beings, landscape, animals, architecture, or a combination of some or all of these) is meant to signify the harmonious order of the Kingdom to come. It is not the "integrity of creation" here and now with which the icon — or the Christian — is primarily concerned, but rather the integrity of the transfigured creation, when the mineral, vegetable, and animal orders come to participate through human holiness in the divine glory. (That, of course, is not a reason for depreciating natural ecology, but precisely the opposite: an additional ground of concern for it.[166])

The icon tells us not of the wisdom of the world but of the folly of God in the re-creating love that took him to the Cross. It speaks of the new order of the new creation, unheard-of joy when the sufferings of Christ — and (empowered by him) the ascesis of the saints — grant victory over sin and death.

Conclusion

To reiterate, it is not that the Byzantine-Slav icon alone can open to us, in an evangelical and catholic way, a painterly vision of the Kingdom. Here the present author must part company with Ouspensky, in the latter's narrowing of sympathies. Nonetheless, the art that Ouspensky lovingly practiced and described is, providentially, so exemplary a version of what the Gospel art, the art of the Church, should be that it functions as a criterion — a touchstone — for all Christian art in whatever style.

Whatever ritual Church we belong to — whether we be Latins or Syrians or Copts — we can only draw spiritual benefit from exposure to the art of the icon. (The same is true for readers who belong to the ecclesial communities outside the Great Church, though among the Reformed, who issue from an iconoclastic Christianity, this is counsel that will fall, by and large — the Community of Taizé is an exception — on deaf ears.) At a time when there is a dearth of ecclesially minded visual artists in Catholicism, Ouspensky's writings should awaken eyes as well as hearts to his message, both written and painted, of transfigured life in Christ.

EIGHT

Looking to the Other
Jules Monchanin and the Love of the Trinity

Origins

Jules Monchanin was a pioneer of a deeper Christian engage-ment with the Hindu spirituality of India. That was an example, in simply human terms, of "listening to the other" (with a lower-case "o"). But in his case, another dimension of sensibility was involved. Such "listening" was incomplete so long as it was unac-companied by a "looking to the Other" (with an upper case "O"), a looking to the Holy Trinity, who alone could throw light on the depths of India's — often misrepresented — mystical experience.

His younger confrère and fellow Frenchman Henri Le Saux would take this approach further("from Vedanta to the Trinity"). Writing under the Sanskrit monastic name Abhishiktananda, he enjoyed an enviable mastery of the Hindu scriptures. At the same time, however, Abhishiktananda embarked on a more perilous journey, lacking at times the sureness and discretion of Moncha-nin's theological touch. For a while, Le Saux's celebrity overshad-owed that of the older man. But in recent years, prompted in part by the centenary of his birth in 1995, Monchanin's reputa-tion has enjoyed a well-merited revival.

Who was Jules Monchanin? He was born a sickly child into a well-to-do family of vine-growers in the Beaujolais — a well-known wine-producing region of eastern France. The Monchanin household, it has to be said, was rather narrow in its Catholic outlook. Devotees of the cult of St. Joan of Arc, parents and close relatives were patriotic, conservative, pro-clerical, and anti-Dreyfusard — with the notable exception of Jules's maternal grandfather, a liberal agnostic. Asthmatic, the boy had tutors at home, and he was thrown together often with his grandfather, from whom he would draw not, to be sure, doubt about the truth of revelation but rather amplitude of cultural sympathies. However, it would be wrong to give the impression that the parents were philistines. M. Monchanin subscribed to scientific journals. Mme. Monchanin passed on to her son and daughter her love of the French Romantic poets (Lamartine had lived nearby, though the Symbolists Rimbaud and Mallarmé would be more to Jules's taste) as well as practical musicianship. There were huge pools of solitude in the boy's day: to this he would later ascribe the development of his contemplative side and aptitude for speculative thought.

Approach to Priesthood

Religiously fervent, Jules began to think of priesthood at the age of twelve or thirteen. But indifferent to the Liturgy, with little feeling for the Savior or the Mother of the Lord, and hardly more for God as Creator or Father, his Catholicism was curious to say the least. It resembled the philosophy of Plotinus more than it did the Gospel: alone with the Alone.

As if by way of compensation, Jules's powers of critical observation — not least of other people — developed early. After a disastrous attempt to integrate him into a normal boarding school, his parents sent him in 1912 to the school of the minor seminary of Lyons (themselves taking a flat in the city for regular supportive visits). The following year, he transferred to the *grand séminaire* at Francheville — the "cage of crows," as he dubbed it, though the philosophical and theological formation given by priests of the Society of St. Sulpice was by no means bad.

An enthusiast, at first, for the Thomist revival, Monchanin would eventually transfer his allegiance to the Greek Fathers — above all Gregory of Nyssa and, behind him, Origen. Philosophically, he was charmed by the personalist writers — who were somewhat under a cloud in ecclesiastical officialdom owing to their comparative weakness as providers of a general metaphysic for the support of faith.[167] In the aftermath of the Modernist crisis, it was extremely rare for seminarians to be given the free range of the libraries of their institutions. But Monchanin was esteemed and trusted — though, with the outbreak of the First World War, his pacifism and, after the Bolshevik Revolution, sympathy for Trotskyite socialism, strained the confidence of his superiors.

All seminarians, even asthmatic ones, had to do war work. Monchanin's was to be a (not terribly successful) schoolmaster. But this was also the period when under his sister's influence he discovered the Carmelite mystics, notably (to begin with) Thérèse of Lisieux and her younger contemporary Blessed Elizabeth of Dijon, whose Trinitarian mysticism carries affinities to his own. To these names, he would shortly add those of St. John of the Cross and the Flemish mystic Blessed Jan Ruysbroeck, both to be lifelong companions of his prayers.

The Mystery of the Trinity

Unsurprisingly, in one undergoing formation for the priesthood, his religious outlook was becoming more truly Catholic. The mystery of the Trinity would be for him the key to personality, to interiority, to mysticism (including the mysticism, as yet barely known to him, of India), and indeed to being at large. To Monchanin, an ontology — a metaphysics of being — that has learned from the being of the

Holy Trinity will be a meditation not just on *esse* (being, as it were, for itself) but also on *esse ad* ("being toward," which means *being for another*). He called this a "metaphysics of communion":

> In a metaphysics of communion, where *co-esse* is first in relation to *esse*, being is not only diffusive, but is *diffusivity*. Being is, only through its relationship of communion: *Esse* is interior to *co-esse*.

Furthermore, since true communion is a communion of persons, true being — the fullest kind of being — is person:

> Person is 'diffusive' of itself through love; and it is at least radical love which constitutes person in so far as it is person (*esse ad alium*) ["being towards another someone"]. The *co-esse* of persons is communion according to love, and it is within this *co-esse* that the person is person.[168]

At the same time, he was reading Nietzsche, Marx, Jung (entirely predictable in the Paris of the 1960s, but at Saint-Gildas de Charlieu in 1916?), and the Indian philosophers, of whom the latter — though Monchanin did not know it then — would mark his life.

The Mystery of the Other

Meanwhile, friendship with a fellow-ordinand, Edouard Duperray, a painter, opened Monchanin's eyes to the visual arts — and more. (Duperray will write the first memoir of Monchanin's life and, thirty-three years after Monchanin's death, be buried with him in the same grave.[169]) Together, as young soutane-clad abbés, they sought out Picasso for a personal interview — a parable of the omnivorously enquiring attitude to novelty in contemporary culture, which became a Monchanin hallmark. Listening to (or looking at) the other, Monchanin hoped to find there some alien echo of the Gospel and the faith. Moreover, the love of friendship — found in Duperray, it seems, for the first time — dissolves a certain cerebral egoism in him. Here, too, is the opening out to otherness. Monchanin later wrote of the love of spouses:

> Love inscribes in the flesh a metaphysical thirst for the other. It breaks the ring of solitude of the monad enclosed in its ipseity [selfhood]. By its very presence, love rejects the desolate vision of the melancholy thinker who projects on consciousness the incommunicability characteristic of his own enclosed consciousness. The other [person], chosen, contemplated, and loved in her very otherness, in her essential mystery, becomes the pole, the force of attraction. This communion without fusion, communion that, instead, sharpens differences and completes the identity of each person according to her own axis, always threatened and continually overcoming the monotony and confusion of daily life, growing deeper as it is spiritualized with the passing of time: this is the miracle of love. Transposed from one's spouse to God: this is the mystery of holiness.[170]

Ordination and Beyond

In 1922, Jules Monchanin was ordained on the feast of Sts. Peter and Paul in Lyons cathedral. Chosen from among the *neo-ordinati* to give the word of thanks to their old professors, he showed that, whatever his other enthusiasms, he had picked up the essentials from the Sulpicians, whose spirituality was deeply embedded in the masters of the seventeenth-century "French School." Thanking his teachers, he remarked:

Theology, freed at least from vain disputes [probably a reference to Modernism and Anti-Modernism], struck us as a life, and the most poignant of lives: that of Christ in his Incarnation and in each of our souls.[171]

In point of fact, Monchanin will prefer the mystics to the theologians: better to experience the mystery of God than to construct a doctrine of God. (Not for nothing would the first published collection of his scattered writings be titled "From Aesthetics to Mysticism," though the title was Duperray's choosing.[172])

The charism of an intellectual mystic did not sit well, unfortunately, with his chosen research work: on the nature of membership of the Church. Sensing its discord with the more sober Catholic ecclesiology then in favor (he proposed a "pan-Christic" scheme, whereby, through the work of the Holy Spirit, all human beings could be said to bear a relation to the Church considered as the pleroma, or "fullness," of Christ, consummation of the creation), he did not persevere with his thesis.

Still, higher studies at the Institut Catholique de Lyon were not all a waste of time. Monchanin further broadened his already wide culture, as well as his contacts with politicians, liturgists, and theologians — although it would not be until 1930 that he would meet Henri de Lubac, star of the great Jesuit school of theology at Lyon-Fourvières and future inspirer of that forerunner of the Second Vatican Council, the *Nouvelle Théologie*. (De Lubac was so impressed with Monchanin that he devoted a book to him after Monchanin's death, and De Lubac's *Memoirs* treated him as both mystic and saint.[173])

All the same, Monchanin's pastoral solicitude was a good deal more adventurous than that normally expected of a curate — concern for the miners of the Lyons coalfield, Communists, and tramps; for émigré students from the old Russia; and for doctors and philosophers worrying over medical ethics. But increasingly, letters and biographical fragments told of one privileged theme: Sanskrit, the Upanishads (principal mystical-philosophical commentaries on the original Hindu scriptures, the Vedic hymns) — in a word, India. Falling seriously ill in the winter of 1932, Monchanin made a vow to God that, if he recovered, he would go to India — for good. Owing to the opposition of successive archbishops at home and the difficulty of finding a new bishop to incardinate him abroad, the dream would not be realized for the better part of a decade. He would be forty-five when he first stepped onto Indian soil. Yet India was the thread that never ceased to guide him through the labyrinth.

On the Frontiers

And what a labyrinth Monchanin made of life! He saw himself as a priest "for the frontiers." He headed for the places and people where Christ and the Church were barely named, the Spirit unacknowledged. On those frontiers, he found, among others:

- Chinese Buddhist students, whom he engaged in dialogue along with his friend Duperray (who would spend his own middle years in China until the Communists expelled him).
- Members of the Jewish community in Lyons and Paris; a pioneer in Catholic-Jewish relations, Monchanin never sacrificed the place of the Hebrew Bible and Israel's sharp sense of divine transcendence to *rapprochement* with Hindus.
- The social radicals linked with the "personalist communitarian" journal *Esprit*.
- North African Muslims, whom the noted Islamologist Louis Massignon helped Monchanin to understand.

- Fellow Christians, including Orthodox priests and Prot-
  estant pastors (in early ecumenical circles, the themes of
  Monchanin's public speaking — the Trinity, the pleroma
  of the Mystical Body, mission to the other, and the consequent transfiguration of Christendom — would long be
  remembered), members of the Byzantine-Catholic "monasteries of union" (Amay and Chevetogne), the (Catholic
  and Reformed) Groupe de Dombes, and the Calvinist
  founders of the ecumenically minded community at Taizé.

Monchanin's work aimed at ecclesial creativity, but of the
kind the French call *à la longue haleine* ("with the long breath" —
so long-term as to require plenty of puff). The young women to
whom he communicated his spirituality formed a "missionary
circle" that would lead a number of them overseas, to Morocco,
Algeria, and China. He warned them of a future when the visible
Church would be unable to sustain them, when those for whose
sake they are going would not understand them, and when God
would be silent: "Long, till death perhaps, will last your night."[174]
The themes he taught were, above all, the mystery of the Trinity
and openness to all that is good, however strange, in other cul-
tures (for the latter, the example of Charles de Foucauld, the "hermit of the Sahara," was crucial for him). The two motifs were
connected: Love of the other has a Trinitarian root.

> The Trinity is the mystery of the Godhead elucidating itself
> in Otherness (*l'Altérité*), completing itself and returning in
> the other Alterity of unitive Love.[175]

Each member of his missionary circle took a new name in
function of the country where they hoped to serve: Monchanin's

was *Purush*, Sanskrit for "Man," and cognate with *Purusha*, the Absolute, the Unconditioned. Man *and* God: not either/or.

Bound for India

In the summer of 1939, Monchanin was ready to depart. Archbishop Gerlier of Lyons had signed his "exeat" from the diocese. In Tamil Nadu — a land made hallowed for him by the memory of the sixteenth-century Italian Jesuit Robert de Nobili, "Apostle of the Brahmins" — Bishop Mendonça of Trichy (or Trichinopoly, now Tiruchchirappalli), a native Indian, agreed to accept him into his presbyterium. At the Louvain study house of the Auxiliaires de la Mission, Monchanin gathered his thoughts. Obscurely, he was to prepare the Parousia of Christ in India:

> Christ appareled in the glory of India . . . , having assumed all India's values, in him at last purified, unified, taken beyond their own essence (*trans-essenciées*).[176]

Monchanin would found an ashram (an Indian eremitical settlement) dedicated to the Holy Trinity. From the hymns of a Hindu convert to Christianity, Brahmabandhab Upadhyay, he named the Trinity in Sanskrit *Sat-Cit-Ananada* ("Being-Thought-Bliss [or Joy]"). This would be the ashram's title, too. Embarking on a ship at Marseilles, he told a journalist (possibly, suggests Françoise Jacquin, this was a thinly disguised Edouard Duperray!) of his intent

> not to adapt by way of tactics to the customs of India, but to assimilate by love what India has that is essential in the modes of its spiritual experience, in its thought, sensibility, consecrated life. . . .

He added:

> A Christianity which would appear to be purely active, de-
> capitated of its essential function which is to adore and praise
> God, would seem inferior to the indigenous religions.[177]

(This comment picked up one of Monchanin's favored sayings: "The value of a life is its weight of adoration.") Arriving at
Bombay, he traveled by train via Goa and reached Madras, the
capital of the province, on Trinity Sunday.

The Swami

Monchanin's time in India fell into two segments. In the first, he,
one of the best-known priests in France, was the humblest of cu-
rates in village assignments given him by his bishop while he en-
deavored to learn the Tamil language (and afterward). True, he was
not entirely immersed in the basic pastoral work of the hamlets
and small towns of central Tamil Nadu, with its rolling hills and
historic Saivite temples. There was much to learn — not least from
the autochthonous clergy, who, however, knew, and wished to know,
little of Hinduism and, in reaction against native Indian styles,
preferred the artistic manner of nineteenth-century France. For
Monchanin, an inveterate letter-writer, the rupture of postal relations with France and North Africa occasioned by the Second World
War was a cross to bear. It was fortunate that, as will soon become
apparent, his bishop was sympathetic.

Some days after Indian Independence (August 15, 1947), a
letter arrived from France that at last made the foundation of the
ashram possible. A monk of Kergonan (Brittany), enthused by
references to Monchanin's spirituality of mission in an article by
Jean Daniélou (like De Lubac, Daniélou was a Jesuit, a practitio-

ner of *nouvelle théologie,* and a future cardinal), wished to join forces. This was Dom Henri Le Saux, the future Abhishiktananda. Monchanin replied, "filled with the Holy Spirit," telling him of the three gifts he would need: courage, renunciation (of the West), and love (of India). Two years later (in post-colonial India, it was not so easy for a Catholic priest to gain an entry permit), Le Saux arrived, eager to initiate Monchanin into Benedictine monastic life, in exchange for his own initiation into Indian life. With the bishop's consent, the ashram of Shantivanam ("Grove of Peace") was born. It would marry elements of the Hindu ascetic discipline to Christian monasticism in something of the way the latter had espoused Late Ancient Stoic- and Platonic-inspired ways of living. And so, a new, second phase opened for Monchanin.

It would be consoling to report that this partnership was a runaway success. But Monchanin's counsel to his women missionaries was only too right. The limits of local sympathy for the project were exacerbated by the temperamental and indeed ideological differences between the two monks (of whom only one was canonically a monastic). Monchanin saw it as only the *preparation* for a monastic life (and Church) that would be "fully Christian, fully Indian." He felt that two Europeans, by themselves, could hardly do more than "prepare."

So, for Monchanin, it was compatible with this commitment to take time off to give lectures at the French Institute of Indology at Pondicherry (which ceased to be a French colony during his time in the region), and to take part in missionary congresses and the like. As with an Indian Christian theology, the road ahead was long, and shortcuts were of no avail.

Le Saux's attitude was quite different. He thirsted for a facsimile of the life of the most advanced Hindu ascetics here and now.

Similarly, he was happy, intellectually, to embrace *advaita* (the classical "non-dual" Hindu thinking for which there is, ultimately, no otherness between divine and non-divine), holding that such a philosophy could be considered crowned by Trinitarian faith. Not that he could furnish a satisfactory theological explanation of how that might be so. That, Le Saux thought, would have to come later.

Monchanin was content to be a John the Baptist, not seeing clearly the salvific way ahead. Abhishiktananda, for all his profound spirituality, was not. Monchanin wrote:

> Hindu thought, so deeply focused on the Oneness of the One . . . , cannot be sublimated into Trinitarian thought without a crucifying dark night of the soul. It has to undergo a noetic metamorphosis [meaning an intellectual shift of seismic proportions], a passion of the spirit.[178]

Meanwhile:

> Our task is to keep all doors open, to wait with patience and theological hope for the hour of the advent of India into the Church, in order to realize the fullness of the Church and the fullness of India. In this age-long vigil, let us remember that *amor intrat ubi intellectus stat ad ostium*: Love can enter where the intellect must stand at the door.[179]

Waiting on God

His waiting would, at least on earth, not be so long. Despite the painful differences with Abhishiktananda, his last Epiphany at Shantivanam was beautiful. Dom Le Saux described it to his Benedictine sister, back in Brittany: a High Mass, followed by a dinner with Hindu friends and a Muslim:

We all ate together in the same *mandapam* [open porch], after closing the doors of the sanctuary. They made splendid 'Wise Men of the East', don't you think?[180]

The uncertainties over Shantivanam may have overshadowed his last months and years (in fact, Abhishiktananda would continue it until 1968, when Bede Griffiths, a monk of Prinknash, took it over). But given the lack of serious medical attention to the ascetics' health, Monchanin's destiny was sealed by the onset of the (treatable, but, if not treated, fatal) tropical disease kala-azar. Brought on by malnutrition, it can be difficult to distinguish from leukemia. For consolation in his sickness, he read his favorite Western mystics, as well as Balthasar's *Le chrétien Bernanos*, which put him in mind of the ills of the world, Marian compassion, and the grace that "makes the darkness open out into the light."[181]

Against his better judgment (but he was mollified by the Indian government's promise he could return to India), Monchanin was persuaded to go back to France for medical help. Surgery in a Parisian hospital soon proved that the tumors had spread too far. Friends pressed around, the cream of the French Catholic intelligentsia among them.

Someone put by his bed an unusual medallion of the Trinity. Designed by a Polish Jew, it showed the crucified Son lying across the lap of a Father otherwise visible only by his shoulders. The water and fire of the Spirit framed the scene.

On October 10, 1957, with his arms spread out in the shape of a cross (this followed the custom of the Lyonese rite for the Mass celebrant after the Consecration), Jules Monchanin entered that mystery he had loved and served.

III. A SPIRITUALITY FOR THE TWENTY-FIRST CENTURY

Can we now turn the lessons learned sev-
erally, from each of these eight, with their
distinctive messages, into a single whole? I
believe that their sum *does* provide us with
the outline of a spirituality worth the name.

It is right to begin with simplicity — summed up in the Little Way of spiritual childhood of St. Thérèse of Lisieux. In the turbulent seas of twenty-first-century society and life, Christian craft are likely to founder unless their lines are clear and clean, well suited for cleaving the water ahead. A world that presses sophistication on its biological children far too early has need of adults who preserve the spirit of true childhood, in its trust of the loving Father, and openness of heart to all good. Such simplicity is a basic presupposition for all that follows in this spirituality for the new millennium.

That simplicity, though, must enter into and — yes, let us dare to use the word in this context — *master* the complex vastness of the divine plan. The Church's doctrine opens to us endless horizons, but the horizons do not overarch empty space. That space is filled with the figures and events that make up the saving drama of Israel, Christ, and the Church. The Church's doctrines form a cat's nest of interlocking threads, a "nexus of mysteries," as the First Vatican Council called them. Their key is found in the Church's access to Jesus Christ as the Trinitarian Son, revelation on earth of the Blessed Trinity. All of that is made known to us in the sacred Liturgy, where we celebrate the glory of God revealed in that drama's terrible beauty and where we learn to live "doxologically," for the praise of God's glory. That, we saw, was the contribution of Columba Marmion.

We learn there, in the Liturgy, the "shape" — the basic outlines — of the grace of Christ. But putting it into practice in our own lives means developing the right form of human response. That requires the virtues — in their multiplicity and their unity.

It involves the habitual inclinations that go with basic human decency. It also entails the more far-reaching dispositions that belong to the movement toward beatitude. The modern world — as well as the modern Church — has to relearn them. No biography, no community, can do without them if it is to be even in part a carrier of spirituality. G. K. Chesterton was our guide to that.

At least in the West, the twentieth century ended in a fiasco — the aborted "celebration" of the bi-millennium of the Incarnation, and a replacement festival of neophilia, the love of the deracinated for the as-yet-unknown "new." In this situation, no Christian spirituality can survive without particular attention to the theological virtue of hope. That is why I included Charles Péguy among our octet.

But if hope is to be more than "hoping against hope," it must be informed by a Christian intelligence. In an ideologically hostile world, the spirituality of the future will cut no ice unless it is thoughtful and, as the First Letter of Peter has it, "prepared to make a defense to any one who calls you to account for the hope that is in you" (3:15). A Catholic faith should be, according to the measure possible for each individual, not only an informed faith but also a reflective faith that ponders the Creed and the other teachings of Tradition, so as to become truly wise. For the early Fathers, the Christian was the true philosopher — so long as, at any rate, he or she truly loved wisdom. That is the message, too, of St. Edith Stein, the professional philosopher who learned the science of the Cross.

But Edith Stein was not only concerned with the truth-finding of individuals. She also struggled for the soul of Germany, just as she gave her life as an offering for her people Israel. Although our first duty is to evangelize ourselves, we cannot forget the needs of the human city — not least because our ultimate goal is to share in the life of that city transfigured, in the City of God. In the Church, which is the sacrament of that City, we rehearse the life that will be all the vitality of the final City by learning to bear one another's burdens. Charles Williams is the mystic of this. It is no mere social Gospel we have to deal with, but a vision of co-inherence that goes right back through the substitutionary sacrifice of the Atonement into the heart of the Holy Trinity.

This is hard, unrelenting soul-work. And if we are to stick it with it to the end, we will need, while we are on the way, momentary glimpses of the Glory that is to come. A Church that lacks iconic beauty cannot sustain us on our pilgrimage. It will have no power to refresh us on the dusty trek through an often-soulless world. That is where Leonid Ouspensky came in, to teach us his particular lesson. The Church becomes just another organization unless its consciousness is pierced through and through by the beauty shown in the icons. This is the wonder that entered the world with the Incarnation, and which is taking the world beyond the marvels of creation to transfigured existence in the Uncreated Light of God.

Finally, a Catholic spirituality for the twenty-first century cannot afford to be narrow. In a world that is shrinking, thanks to the revolutions of transport and communication as well as the movement of peoples, the spirituality of the Church must not come across as that of a sect. Rather, it must show that, with full confidence, it can look the "other" in the face, whoever that other may be. And so looking, it must be able to descry in that face whatever in the mysteries of creation and grace are still hid from the Church, because not all who are on the way to the Kingdom can be found in the ranks of the baptized. That will entail neither the denaturing nor the dilution of Catholic Christianity. It will not mean an attempt to pour all world religions as ingredients into a pan-religious soup. It will not involve fashioning a lowest common denominator of the opinions of Everyman. Instead, it will signify the repatriation to the Church (as Christ's Mystical Body) of all that belongs (within or without her visible confines) to the Lord's fullness. That is not the blithe welcome — just as they are — of anything. On the contrary, it requires a demanding asceticism that renounces much of the comfortingly familiar, the better to essay a serious discernment of the value of the other. In so doing, as Jules Monchanin saw, it whores after no strange gods but re-finds that mystery of identity in otherness, which is the Trinity itself.

Glory to Them — to Him!

NOTES

1. John Paul II, *Lettre apostolique "Divini amoris scientia," Proclamation de Sainte Thérèse de l'Enfant-Jesus et de la Sainte-Face Docteur de l'Eglise universelle* (Paris, 1997).

2. P. Descovremont, *Therese and Lisieux* (English translation [hereafter "E.t."] Dublin and Grand Rapids, Mich., 1996), p. 72. I have based the biographical elements in this chapter chiefly on this richly illustrated work. But see also the standard life: G. Gaucher, *Histoire d'une vie, Thérèse Martin, 1973-1897, Soeur Thérèse de l'Enfant-Jésus et de la Sainte-Face* (Paris, 1997; new edition).

3. See the essays in J. Baudry, O.C.D. (ed.), *Thérèse et ses théologiens* (Versailles-Venasque, 1998), and also the collection *Thérèse au milieu des docteurs* (Venasque, 1998).

4. Thérèse de l'Enfant Jésus et de la Sainte-Face, *La première "Histoire d'une Ame" de 1898, texte intégral des 11 premiers chapitres, dans la version de Mère Agnès de Jésus* (Paris, 1992). For the complicated redactional history, see C. de Meester, O.C.D., "De la cellule de Thérèse de Lisieux à l'atelier de l'imprimeur. Le tout début de *L'Histoire d'une Ame*," in J. Baudry, O.C.D. (ed.), *Thérèse et ses théologiens*, op. cit., pp.13-51.

5. Now superseded by Thérèse de l'Enfant-Jésus et de la Sainte-Face, *Manuscrits autobiographiques. Edition critique* (Paris, 1992).

6. F. de Sainte-Marie, *Le Visage de Thérèse de Lisieux* (Lisieux, 1961; 2 volumes).

7. Later republished in two volumes: *Derniers Entretiens avecs ses soeurs, Mère Agnès de Jésus, Soeur Geneviève, Soeur Marie du Sacré-Coeur et Témoignages divers, Deuxième édition revue et corrigée,* and *Dernieres paroles. Toutes les Paroles recueillies pendant les six derniers mois. Synopse des quatre versions des Derniers entretiens de Mère Agnès*

de Jésus. Variantes et témoignages divers, Deuxième édition revue et corrigée ([both] Paris, 1992).

8. E. Przywara, S.J., *Heroisch* (Paderborn, 1936); *Humanitas* (Nuremberg, 1952); see further, E.M. Faber, "Le chemin de kénose: la réponse de sainte Thérèse à l'héroïsme de ses contemporains d'après le Père Erich Przywara, S.J.," in J. Baudry, O.C.D. (ed.), *Thérèse et ses théologiens*, op. cit., pp.95-108. Following in Przywata's footsteps is N. Hausman, *Frédéric Nietzsche, Thérèse de Lisieux. Deux poétiques de la modernité* (Paris, 1984), pp. 73-100.

9. P. Descouvemont, *Therese and Lisieux*, op. cit., p. 225.

10. See G. Gaucher, *John and Thérèse: Flames of Love: The Influence of St. John of the Cross in the Life and Writings of St. Thérèse of Lisieux* (E.t. Staten Island, N.Y., 1999).

11. *Autobiography of a Saint: Thérèse of Lisieux* (London, 1958), p. 127.

12. Ibid., p. 221.

13. N.D. O'Donoghue, O.C.D., "The Paradox of Prayer," *Doctrine and Life* (January 1974), p. 36.

14. *Autobiography of a Saint,* op. cit., p. 217.

15. Ibid., p. 235. This is the famous passage in the *Autobiography*, actually from Manuscript B, that she wrote for her sister Pauline (Sister Marie of the Sacred Heart), who was also her godmother and had asked for a summary of her doctrine.

16. For the evolution of her convictions concerning her role after death, see C. O'Donnell, O.Carm., *Love in the Heart of the Church: The Mission of Thérèse of Lisieux* (Dublin, 1997), pp. 64-66.

17. Cited by Bishop Guy Gaucher, O.C.D., "Preface," in P. Descouvemont, *Therese and Lisieux*, op. cit., p. 6.

18. Ibid., p. 290.

19. For a rather fuller account of Marmion's life story, see A. Nichols, O. P., "Monks: The Spiritual Doctrine of Columba Marmion," in idem, *Beyond the Blue Glass: Catholic Essays on Faith and Culture*, II (London, 2002), pp. 141-149.

20. The monks of La Pierre-qui-vive, in flight from official anti-clericalism in France, had a *pied-à-terre* at Leopardstown, but no intention of admitting Irish novices.

21. Cited in Dom R. Thibaut, *Abbot Columba Marmion: A Master of the Spiritual Life, 1853-1923* (E.t. London and Edinburgh, 1932), p. 30. A classic biography, by the editor of Marmion's conferences, and full of spirited and prescient judgments.

22. Cited in M. Tierney, O.S.B., *Dom Columba Marmion: A Biography* (Blackrock, Co. Dublin, 1994), p. 42. This new biography makes use of many manuscript sources uncovered in the course of preparing Marmion's cause of canonization, as well as in its author's own research.

23. Columba Marmion, *Le Christ vie de l'âme* (Maredsous, 1914, recte, 1917; E.t. London, 1922); idem, *Le Christ dans ses mystères* (Tamines, 1919; E.t. London, 1924); idem, *Le Christ, idéal du moine* (Maredsous, 1922; E.t. London, 1926). Also important are his spiritual letters, of which a selection has been published as *Union with God* (E.t. London, 1935) and *The English Letters of Abbot Marmion, 1858-1923* (Baltimore, 1962). A full bibliography is provided in M. Tierny, O.S.B., *Dom Columba Marmion*, pp. 278-280.

24. Idem, *Christ the Life of the Soul*, p. 7.

25. Ibid., p. 44. Here, Marmion looks forward to the material he will present in the midway work of the trilogy, *Christ in His Mysteries*.

26. Ibid., p. 64.

27. Ibid., p.110; *Tu solus sanctus, Jesu Christe* ("You alone are holy, Jesus Christ").

28. Ibid., p. 451.

29. Ibid., p.452.

30. Ibid., p. 307.

31. Ibid., p. 308.

32. As in his study of that title (Maredsous, 1923; E.t. Glasgow, 1925).

33. Idem, *Christ the Life of the Soul*, op. cit., p. 313.

34. Ibid., pp. 313-314.

35. Ibid., p. 318.

36. Ibid., p. 318. Italics original.

37. Ibid., p. 319.

38. Ibid., p. 321. For another account of the same themes, see idem, *Christ the Ideal of the Monk* (E.t. London, 1926), pp. 294-306.

39. Cf. Dom R. Thibaut, *Abbot Columba Marmion: A Master of the Spiritual Life, 1858-1923* (E.t. London and Edinburgh, 1923), pp. 160-163, where Thibaut explores the "synthetic" quality of Marmion's spirituality.

40. E. Cammaerts, *The Laughing Prophet: The Seven Virtues and G.K. Chesterton* (London, 1937), p.2.

41. This is the theme of David Fagerberg's marvelous study, *The Size of Chesterton's Catholicism* (Notre Dame, Ind., 1998).

42. G.K. Chesterton, *The Resurrection of Rome* (London, 1930), p. 162.

43. Idem, *The Everlasting Man* (London, 1925), p. 300.

44. Idem, *Heretics* (London 1904; 1905, 3rd ed.), p. 286.

45. Idem, *Autobiography* (London, 1936), p. 41.

46. J. Coates, *Chesterton and the Edwardian Cultural Crisis* (Hull, 1984), pp. 1-45.

47. Cited in W. Martin, *The 'New Age' under Orage* (London, 1967), p. 215.

48. G.K. Chesterton, *Orthodoxy* (London 1908; 1996), p. 30.

49. Idem, *The Thing* (London, 1929), p. 26.

50. Ibid., p. 22.

51. Ibid., p. 34.

52. Idem, *Orthodoxy*, op. cit., pp. 34-35.

53. Ibid., p. 166.

54. Idem, *Chaucer: A Study* (London, 1932), pp. 158-159.

55. Idem, *Orthodoxy*, op. cit., p. 167.

56. A. Nichols, O.P., "Chesterton and the Moral Structure of Culture," in idem, *Beyond the Blue Glass: Catholic Essays on Faith and Culture,* II (London, 2002), pp. 65-80.

57. Cf. J. Saward, *The Way of the Lamb: The Spirit of Childhood and the End of the Age* (Edinburgh, 1999), pp. 7-58.

58. G.K. Chesterton, *Orthodoxy*, op. cit., p. 4.

59. Idem, *Christendom in Dublin*, op. cit., p. 13. Had Chesterton lived long enough, he could have found the combination, typical of a Catholic aesthetic, thoroughly exemplified in J.R.R. Tolkien's trilogy, *The Lord of the Rings*, a work which never so much as once mentions Catholicism or revelation.

60. Idem, *Chaucer*, op. cit., p. 275.

61. Ibid., p. 293.

62. P. Fitzgerald, *The Knox Brothers* (London, 1977; 1991), p. 108, citing R.A. Knox, *Some Loose Stones*.

63. J. et J. Tharaud, *Notre cher Péguy*, II (Paris, 1926), p. 18.

64. J.N. Humes, *Two against Time: A Study of the Very Present Worlds of Paul Claudel and Charles Péguy* (Chapel Hill, N.C., 1978), p. 27.

65. R.T. Sussex, *The Sacrificed Generation: Studies of Charles Péguy, Ernest Psichari, and Alain-Fournier* (Townsville, 1980), pp. 22-23.

66. G. Hill, "The Mystery of the Charity of Charles Péguy," in idem, *Collected Poems* (Harmondsworth, 1985), p. 188. The "terre charnelle" refers to Péguy's own makarism (beatitude): Happy are those who die for the land of their flesh, provided the war is just.

67. C. Péguy, *The Portal of the Mystery of Hope*, D.L. Schindler, Jr. (ed.) (Grand Rapids, Mich., and Edinburgh, 1996), Preface, p. xx.

68. Ibid., p. 6.

69. Ibid., p. 72.

70. Ibid., p. 64.

71. Ibid., p. 65.

72. Thomas Aquinas, *Summa Theologiae,* IIa. IIae., q. 17, a. 2, corpus.

73. Ibid., ad ii.

74. In an attempt to explain why Geoffrey Hill is the lodestar of the foremost poet writing in English today, W.S. Milne has written that Péguy attracts because, in his commitment to a life of action as an "enrichment of meditation," he "did not join a political party, or submit to public opinion, parliamentary strategy or economic power; he was more taken up with clarity of thought, patriotism, a sense of mission and a belief in personal sacrifice" — qualities needed for any worthwhile effort

toward the reawakening of Christendom in England today. See W.S. Milne, *An Introduction to Geoffrey Hill* (London, 1998), p. 149.

75. C. Péguy, *The Portal of the Mystery of Hope*, op. cit., p. 119.

76. C. Schönborn, *The Mystery of the Incarnation* (E.t. San Francisco, 1993), p. 48.

77. Various case studies are set out in G. Rutler, *A Crisis of Saints* (San Francisco, 1999).

78. E. Stein, *Life in a Jewish Family: Her Unfinished Autobiographical Account* (E.t. Washington, 1986, part of [hereafter "="] *The Collected Works of Edith Stein*, Vol. I, = Vol. VII of *Edith Steins Werke: Aus dem Leben einer jüdischen Familie* [Freiburg, Basle, Vienna, 1965; 1985]).

79. Ibid., p. 23.

80. Ibid., p. 35. Her own political credo can be found on pp. 190-191: It is patriotism without nationalism, conservatism but of a sort "never tainted by the particular . . . Prussian . . . stamp."

81. Ibid., p. 218.

82. Ibid., p. 244.

83. E. Stein, *Zum Problem der Einfühlung* (Halle, 1917; Munich, 1980).

84. Idem, "Husserls Phänomenologie und die Philosophie des heiligen Thomas von Aquino. Versuch einer Gegenüberstellung," in *Festschrift Edmund Husserl zum 70. Geburtstag gewidmet* [= *Ergänzungsband zum Jahrbuch für Philosophie und phänomenologische Forschung*] (Halle, 1939), pp. 315-338. The mature fruit of this encounter between phenomenology and traditional Christian ontology is found in her great work on "finite and everlasting being," *Endliches und ewiges Sein. Versuch eines Aufstiegs zum Sinn des Seins* [= *Werke*, II] (Freiburg, Basle, Vienna, 1986, 3rd ed.; original 1936).

85. Idem, *Kreuzeswissenschaft. Studie über Joannes a Cruce* [= *Werke*, I] (Druten, Freiburg, Basle, Vienna, 1983, 3rd ed.; original 1942).

86. Idem, "Die ontische Struktur der Person und ihre erkenntnistheoretische Problematik," in *Werke*, VI, pp. 137-197, and here at p. 145.

87. F. Gaboriau, *Lorsque Edith Stein se convertit* (Geneva, 1997); E.t. *The Conversion of Edith Stein* (South Bend, Ind., 2002).

88. R. Leuven, O.C.D., *Heil im Unheil. Das Leben Edith Steins: Reife und Vollendung* (Druten, Freiburg, Basle, Vienna, 1983), pp.30-49.

89. Teresia Renata de Spiritu Sancto, O.C.D., *Edith Stein* (Nuremberg, 1954), p.68.

90. E. Stein, "Die ontische Struktur der Person und ihre erkenntnistheoretische problematik," art. cit., p. 192.

91. Ibid., p. 39.

92. E. Stein, "Was ist Philosophie? Ein Gespräch zwischen Edmund Husserl und Thomas von Aquino," *Werke*, XV. *Erkenntnis und Glaube* (Freiburg, Basle, Vienna, 1993), p.24.

93. Ibid., pp. 32-34.

94. Idem, *Endliches und ewiges Sein. Versuch eines Aufstiegs zum Sinn des Seins* (= *Werke*, II [Freiburg, Basle, Vienna, 1986, 3rd ed.]), p. 30.

95. Ibid., p. 47.

96. Her most thorough and finished philosophical work, *Endliches und ewiges Sein*, op. cit.

97. Idem, *Kreuzeswissenschaft, Studie über Joannes a Cruce* (= *Werke*, I [Druten, Freiburg, Basle, Vienna, 1983, 3rd ed.]).

98. *Des Hl. Thomas von Aquino Untersuchungen über die Wahrheit* (Breslau, 1932; = *Werke*, III/IV [Louvain and Freiburg, 1952-1955]).

99. R.J. Evans, "Anti-Semitism: Ordinary Germans and the 'longest hatred,' " in idem, *Rereading German History, 1800-1996: From Unification to Reunification* (London, 1997), pp. 165-166.

100. R. Leuven, O.C.D., *Heil im Unheil*, op. cit., pp. 170-171.

101. Ibid., p. 182.

102. These passages from the text of the pope's homily are taken from the English-language edition of *L'Osservatore Romano*, October 14, 1998. For the full text, see F. Gaboriau, *The Conversion of Edith Stein*, op. cit., pp. 123-132.

103. G. Cavaliero, *Charles Williams: Poet of Theology* (London and Basingstoke, 1983), p. 1.

104. C. Williams, *He Came Down from Heaven and the Forgiveness of Sins* (London, 1950), p. 30.

105. Fortunately, some help is available in interpreting this complex poetic material: see C.S. Lewis, *Arthurian Torso: Containing the Posthumous Fragment of the 'Figure of Arthur' by Charles Williams, and a Commentary on the Arthurian Poems of Charles Williams* (London, 1948), and also, though much less ambitiously, *Notes on the Taliessin Poems of Charles Williams, by Various Hands* (Oxford, Charles Williams Society, 1991). These "notes" were gradually assembled over the years 1977 to 1986; the "hands" are those of six people who spoke personally with Williams about the poems: Alice Hadfield, Anne Ridler, Anne Scott, Thelma Shuttleworth, and Joan and Richard Wallis.

106. For Williams on evil, see B. Horne, *Imagining Evil* (London, 1996), pp. 104-123.

107. C. Williams, *Witchcraft* (London, 1941; Wellingborough, 1980), p. xix.

108. Idem, *The Descent of the Dove: A Short History of the Holy Spirit in the Church* (London, 1939, 1950), p.vii.

109. Ibid., p. 15.

110. Ibid., p. 10.

111. Ibid., p.25.

112. Ibid., p. 27.

113. Ibid., p. 48.

114. Ibid., pp. 48-49.

115. Ibid., p. 86.

116. Ibid., p. 58.

117. Ibid., p. 59.

118. Ibid., p. 181.

119. Ibid., pp. 107-108.

120. Ibid., p. 114.

121. Ibid., p. 52.

122. Ibid., p. 39.

123. Ibid., pp. 69-70.

124. Idem, *He Came Down from Heaven and the Forgiveness of Sins*, op. cit., p. 24.

125. Idem, *The Descent of the Dove*, op. cit., p. 235.

126. Idem, *He Came Down from Heaven and the Forgiveness of Sins*, op., cit., pp. 92, 93, and 94.

127. Ibid., p. 115.

128. Ibid., p. 46, with a citation of John 17:21.

129. Ibid., p. 71.

130. Ibid., pp. 73-74.

131. Cited in A. Ridler, "Introduction," in C. Williams, *The Image of the City and Other Essays* (London, 1958), p. xv.

132. Idem, *The Descent of the Dove,* op. cit., p. 75.

133. Idem, *The Region of the Summer Stars* (London, 1944), pp. 54-55.

134. Idem, *The Descent of the Dove,* op. cit., p. 84.

135. Idem, *He Came Down from Heaven and the Forgiveness of Sins*, op. cit., p. 23.

136. Ibid., p. 36.

137. Idem, *The Descent of the Dove,* op. cit., p. 225.

138. Ibid., pp. 229-230.

139. Idem, *Descent into Hell* (London, 1939; Grand Rapids, Mich., 1999), p. 98.

140. Idem, "The Redeemed City," in C. Williams, *The Image of the City and Other Essays*, op. cit., pp. 108-109.

141. Idem, *He Came Down from Heaven and the Forgiveness of Sins*, op. cit., p. 172.

142. Ibid., p. 173.

143. I argue for this in "On Baptizing the Visual Arts: a Friar's Meditation on Art," in A. Nichols, O.P., *Scribe of the Kingdom: Essays on Theology and Culture* (London, 1994), pp. 183-196.

144. H. Belting, *Likeness and Presence: A History of the Image before the Era of Art* (Chicago and London, 1994), pp. 25 and 311; and see pp. 63-73 and 311- 376 for icons, indigenous or imported, in the West.

145. L. Ouspensky, *La théologie de l'icône dans l'Eglise orthodoxe* (Paris, 1980), pp. 234-235. He does not seem to have been aware of the early twentieth-century efforts of the Czardom, urged on by such devout scholars as S. Sheremetev, to return to the original sources of the Russian icon (and end the production of paper and "tinplate" copies of sometimes rather decadent models). See R.L. Nichols, "The Icon and the Machine in Russia's Religious Renaissance, 1900-1909," in W.C. Brumfield and M.M. Velimirovic (eds.), *Christianity and the Arts in Russia* (Cambridge, 1991), pp. 131-144.

146. L. Ouspensky, "Biographie de L. A. Ouspensky," in S. Doolan, *La redécouverte de l'Icône. La vie et l'oeuvre de Léonide Ouspensky* (Paris, 2001), p. 10.

147. Ibid.

148. For the background, see A. Nichols, O.P., *Theology in the Russian Diaspora: Church, Fathers, Eucharist in Nikolai Afanas'ev, 1893-1966* (Cambridge, 1989), pp. 53-57.

149. L. Ouspensky, *Le théologie de l'icône dans l'Eglise orthodoxe*, op. cit., pp. 27-35.

150. Note, however, that elsewhere in his major study, Ouspensky regards the making of icons — considered as expressions of humanity's participation in the sanctification proper to the Christian economy — as impossible until Pentecost. See ibid., p. 153.

151. Idem, "The Meaning and Language of Icons," in L. Ouspensky and V. Lossky, *The Meaning of Icons* (Crestwood, N.Y., 1982), p. 25.

152. C.P. Kelley, "Canterbury's First Ikon," *Bulletin of the Friends of Canterbury Cathedral,* 1977, pp. 41-44, cited in R.A. Markus, "The Cult of Icons in Sixth Century Gaul," in idem, *From Augustine to Gregory the Great* (London, 1983), XII., p. 157.

153. A document that forms part of the seventeenth-century Russian debate over the principles of Church art, *The Writing of the Three Patriarchs*, shows that Easterners also became aware of the "Vernicle," probably around this date: thus, L. Ouspensky, *La théologie de l'icône dans l'Eglise orthodoxe* , op. cit., p. 319, n. 50.

154. Idem, "The Meaning and Language of Icons," art. cit., p. 27. Ouspensky's evaluation of the art of the catacombs is much indebted to a Russian historian of Christian art working under the Soviets: V.N. Lazarev, and notably his "History of Byzantine Painting," *Istoriya vizantiiskoi zhivopisi* (Moscow, 1947).

155. The text is conveniently available in C. Mango, *The Art of the Byzantine Empire, 312-1453: Sources and Documents* (Englewood Cliffs, N.J., 1972), pp. 139-140. Ouspensky discusses its implications, and the vexed question of its Western "reception," in *La théologie de l'icône dans l'Eglise orthodoxe,* op. cit., pp. 72-81.

156. Ibid., pp. 59-64.

157. Ibid., p. 121.

158. Ibid., pp. 121-122.

159. This whole issue occupies the lion's share of Ouspensky's attention in his treatment of Russian Orthodox iconographical doctrine and trends in ibid., pp.260-386. His exegesis of the Triumph of Orthodoxy kontakion on pp. 134-137 of *La théologie de l'icône* both reflects and dictates his opposition to such theologians of the icon as Sergei Bulgakov, who were happy to accept the "Paternity" icon.

160. Ibid., p. 139.

161. Diadochus of Photike, *Oeuvres spirituelles* (Paris, 1955), p. 149.

162. S. Doolan, *La redécouverte de l'Icône,* op. cit., pp. 73 and 52.

163. L. Ouspensky, *La théologie de l'icône,* op. cit., pp. 143 and 144.

164. Ibid., pp. 145-146.

165. Ibid., p. 169.

166. See A. Nichols, O.P., "Recentring on the End," in idem, *Christendom Awake: On Re-energising the Church in Culture* (Grand Rapids, Mich., and Edinburgh, 1999), pp. 219-232.

167. For a fuller account of Monchanin's early intellectual enthusiasms, see F. Jacquin, *Jules Monchanin, prêtre* (Paris, 1996), pp. 25-47. It is not surprising that the rigors of the Anti-Modernist oath caused him some searching of conscience.

168. J. Monchanin, "Creation," in J.G. Weber (ed.), *In Quest of the Absolute: The Life and Work of Jules Monchanin* (Kalamazoo, Mich., and London, 1977), p. 148.

169. E. Duperray, *L'Abbé Jules Monchanin* (Bruges, 1956).

170. J. Monchanin, "Notes," in J. Weber (ed.), *In Quest of the Absolute*, op. cit., p. 117. (Translation slightly altered.)

171. Cited in F. Jacquin, *Jules Monchanin, prêtre*, op. cit., p. 46.

172. J. Monchanin, *De l'esthétique à la mystique, texte présenté par E. Duperray* (Tournai, 1955; Bruges, 1967).

173. H. de Lubac, *Images de l'abbé Monchanin* (Paris, 1967); idem, *Memoires sur l'occasion de mes livres* (Namur, 1989), p. 114.

174. Cited in F. Jacquin, *Jules Monchanin, prêtre*, op. cit., p. 126.

175. J. Monchanin, "Creation," art. cit., p. 149.

176. Cited in F. Jacquin, *Jules Monchanin, prêtre*, op. cit., p. 163.

177. The interview, originally published in a review of the *Union missionaire du clergé* for July 1939, is reprinted in J. Monchanin, *Théologie et spiritualite missionaire* (Paris, 1985), pp. 194-195.

178. J. Monchanin, "The Quest of the Absolute," in J.G. Weber (ed.), *In Quest of the Absolute*, op. cit., p. 132.

179. Cited from a letter of 1954 in J.G. Weber (ed.), *In Quest of the Absolute*, op. cit., p. 100.

180. Letter of February 7, 1957, cited in J. Stuart, *Swami Abhishiktananda: His Life Told Through His Letters* (New Delhi, 1995), p. 100.

181. Letter of July 10, 1957, cited in F. Jacquin, *Jules Monchanin, prêtre*, op. cit., p. 307.

BIBLIOGRAPHY

Chapter One (Thérèse of Lisieux)

Writings

Oeuvres complètes. Textes et dernières paroles (Paris, 1992).

Autobiography of a Saint: Thérèse of Lisieux (London, 1958).

Story of a Soul: The Autobiography of St. Thérèse of Lisieux (Washington, 1976).

Her Last Conversations (Washington, 1977).

Letters of Saint Thérèse of Lisieux (I, Washington, 1982; II, Washington, 1988).

The Poetry of Saint Thérèse of Lisieux (Washington, 1995).

Secondary Works

Balthasar, H.U. von. Two Sisters in the Spirit: Thérèse of Lisieux and Elizabeth of the Trinity (E.t. San Francisco, 1992).

Bro, B., O.P. La Gloire et le mendiant (Paris, 1975).

De Meester, C., O.C.D. Les mains vides, ma pauvreté devint ma richesse. Le message de Thérèse de Lisieux (Paris, 1994).

_____ Dynamique de la confiance. Génèse et structure de la 'voie d'enfance spirituelle' de sainte Thérèse de Lisieux (Paris, 1995).

Descouvemont, P. Thérèse et Lisieux (Paris, 1991); E.t. Therese and Lisieux (Dublin and Grand Rapids, Mich., 1996).

O'Donnell, C., O.Carm. Love in the Heart of the Church: The Mission of Thérèse of Lisieux (Dublin, 1997).

Petitot, H., O.P. Sainte Thérèse de Lisieux. Une renaissance spirituelle (Paris, 1926, 2nd ed.).

Chapter Two (Columba Marmion)

Writings

Le Christ vie de l'Ame (Maredsous, 1917); E.t. *Christ the Life of the Soul* (London, 1922).

Le Christ dans ses Mystères (Tamines, 1919); E.t. *Christ in His Mysteries* (London, 1924).

Le Christ idéal du moine (Maredsous, 1922); E.t. *Christ the Ideal of the Monk* (London, 1926).

Sponsa Verbi (Paris, 1923); E.t. *Sponsa Verbi* (Glasgow, 1925).

Le Chemin de la Croix (Maredsous, 1923); E.t. *The Way of the Cross* (London, 1923).

L'union à Dieu dans le Christ (Paris, 1934); E.t. *Union with God* (London, 1935).

Paroles de vie en marge du missel (Maredsous, 1937); E.t. *Words of Life* (London, 1940).

Venez au Christ, vous tous qui peiniez (Maredsous, 1941); E.t. *Suffering with Christ* (Westminster, Md., 1952).

Les mystères du Rosaire (Maredsous, 1942); E.t. *The Mysteries of the Rosary* (Marmion Abbey, Aurora, Ill., 1949).

Consécration à la sainte Trinité (Maredous, 1946); E.t. *The Trinity in Our Spiritual Life* (Westminster, Md., 1953).

Le Christ idéal du prêtre (Maredsous, 1951); E.t. *Christ the Ideal of the Priest* (London, 1952).

The English Letters of Abbot Marmion (Dublin, 1963).

"La semaine liturgique francaise, Louvain (7-12 août [1911])," *Revue liturgique et bénédictine I* (1911-1912), pp. 455-466, for a summary of Marmion's three Conferences on the Liturgy.

"Cours et Conferences de la Semaine Liturgique de Maredsous" (19-24 août [1912]) (Maredsous, 1913).

Secondary Works

Delforge, T. *Le serviteur de Dieu, Columba Marmion* (Turnhout 1963); E.t. *Servant of God* (St. Louis, Mo., 1965).

Gorce, D. *A l'école de Dom Columba Marmion* (Bruges, 1942).

Philipon, M.M., O.P. *La doctrine spirituelle de Dom Columba Marmion* (Paris, 1954); E.t. *The Spiritual Doctrine of Dom Marmion* (London, 1956).

Thibaut, R. *Dom Columba Marmion. Un maître de la vie spiri-tuelle* (Maredsous, 1953, 2nd ed.). There is an English translation of the first, 1919, edition: *Dom Columba Marmion: A Master of the Spiritual Life* (London, 1932).

_____ *L'idée maîtresse de la doctrine de Dom Marmion* (Maredsous, 1946).

Tierney, M., O.S.B. *Dom Columba Marmion: A Biography* (Blackrock, Co. Dublin, 1994).

Chapter Three (Gilbert Keith Chesterton)

Writings

The standard bibliography prepared by Chesterton's secretary Dorothy Collins is published in E. Cammaerts, *The Laughing Prophet: The Seven Virtues and G. K. Chesterton* (London, 1937), pp. 233-243; it does not include uncollected essays or, with the exception of the autobiography, posthumously published work. Only works cited in the text above are listed here:

Heretics (London, 1904).
Orthodoxy (London, 1908).
What's Wrong with the World? (London, 1910).
The Everlasting Man (London, 1925).
The Thing: Catholic Essays (London, 1929).
The Resurrection of Rome (London, 1930).
Chaucer: A Study (London, 1932).
Christendom in Dublin (London, 1932).
Autobiography (London, 1936).

A uniform edition of Chesterton's works is being prepared by Ignatius Press, San Francisco, under the title *Collected Works of Chesterton.* At present, it comprises thirty-five volumes, of which

166 A Spirituality for the Twenty-first Century

nos. 27 to 35 consist of contributions to the *Illustrated London News,* 1905-1931.

Secondary Works

Boyd, I. *The Novels of G.K. Chesterton* (London, 1975).
Cammaerts, E. *The Laughing Prophet: The Seven Virtues and G.K. Chesterton* (London, 1937).
Coates, J. *Chesterton and the Edwardian Cultural Crisis* (Hull, 1984).
Fagerberg, D. *The Size of Chesterton's Catholicism* (Notre Dame, Ind., 1998).
Ffinch, M. *G. K. Chesterton* (London, 1986).
Ward, M. *Gilbert Keith Chesterton* (London, 1945).

Chapter Four (Charles Péguy)

Writings

Oeuvre poétique (Paris, 1962).
Oeuvres en prose (2 vols., Paris, 1959-1961).
The Portal of the Mystery of Hope (Grand Rapids, Mich., and Edinburgh, 1996).

Secondary Works

Béguin, A. *La prière de Péguy* (Neuchatel, 1942).
Delaporte, J. *Connaissance de Péguy* (Paris, 1958, 2nd ed.).
Duployé, P. *La Religion de Péguy* (Paris, 1966).
Guyon, B. *Péguy devant Dieu* (Paris, 1974).
Humes, J.N. *Two against Time: A Study of the Very Present Worlds of Paul Claudel and Charles Péguy* (Chapel Hill, N.C., 1978).
Nelson, R.J. *Péguy poète du sacré* (Paris, 1960).
Quoniam, T. *La Pensée de Péguy* (Paris, 1967).
Rousseaux, A. *Le prophète Péguy* (2 vols., Paris, 1946).
St. Aubyn, F.C. *Charles Péguy* (Boston, 1977).
Sussex, R.T. *The Crucified Generation: Studies of Charles Péguy, Ernest Psichari, and Alain-Fournier* (Townsville, 1980), pp. 1-39.

Villiers, M. *Charles Péguy: A Study in Integrity* (London, 1966).

Chapter Five (Edith Stein)

Writings

Edith Steins Werke (Louvain/Druten, Freiburg, Basle, Vienna, 1950-).

"Ways to Know God: The 'Symbolic Theology' of Dionysius the Areopagite and Its Factual Presuppositions," *The Thomist* (1946), pp. 379-420.

Writings of Edith Stein, selected, translated and introduced by Hilda Graef (London, 1956).

Zum Problem der Einfühlung (Halle, 1917; Munich, 1980).

E.t. Complete Works of Edith Stein:

Life in a Jewish Family (Washington, 1987).

Essays on Woman (Washington, 1986).

The Problem of Empathy (Washington, 1990).

The Hidden Life (Washington, 1992).

Self-portrait in Letters, 1916-1942 (Washington, 1993).

Knowledge and Faith (Washington, 2001).

Secondary Works

Bejas, A. *Edith Stein. Von der Phänomenologie zur Mystik. Eine Biographie der Gnade* (Frankfurt, Berne, New York, 1987).

Bouflet, J. *Edith Stein, philosophe crucifiée* (Paris, 1998).

Dubois, M. "L'itinéraire philosophique et spirituel d'Edith Stein," *Revue thomiste* 73 (1973), pp. 181-210.

Elders, L. (ed.). *Edith Stein. Leben, Philosophie, Vollendung* (Würzburg, 1991).

Gaboriau, F. *The Conversion of Edith Stein* (E.t. South Bend, Ind., 2001).

_____ *Edith Stein, philosophe* (Paris, 1989).

Guilead, R. *De la phénoménologie à la science de la Croix. L'itinéraire spirituel d'Edith Stein* (Louvain and Paris, 1974).

Hecker, H. *Phänomenologie des christlichen bei Edith Stein* (Würzburg, 1995).

Herbstrith, W. "Edith Stein, (1891-1942)," in E. Coreth, W.M. Neidl, G. Pfligersdorffer (eds.), *Christliche Philosophie im katholischen Denken des 19. und 20. Jahrhunderts*, II. (Graz and Cologne, 1988), pp. 650-665.

Hofmann, A. *Edith Steins philosophischer Zugang zu Gott in ihrem Werk 'Endliches und ewiges Sein'* (Würzburg, 1977).

Imhof, B.W. *Edith Steins philosophische Entwicklung, Leben und Werk*, I (Basle and Boston, 1987).

Koepcke, C. Edith Stein. *Philosophin und Ordensfrau* (Hamburg and Fribourg, 1985).

Leuven, R., O.C.D. *Heil im Unheil. Das Leben Edith Steins: Reife und Vollendung* (Druten, Freiburg, Basle, Vienna, 1983).

Lyne, P., O.C.D. *Edith Stein: A Personal Portrait* (Leominster, 2000).

Chapter Six (Charles Williams)

Writings

All Hallows Eve (London, 1945).

Descent into Hell (London, 1937).

The Descent of the Dove: A Short History of the Holy Spirit in the Church (London, 1939).

The Figure of Beatrice: A Study in Dante (London, 1943).

The Forgiveness of Sins (London, 1942).

He Came Down from Heaven (London, 1938).

The Image of the City and Other Essays (London, 1958).

The Region of the Summer Stars (London, 1944).

Taliessin through Logres (London, 1938).

Secondary Works

Carpenter, H. *The Inklings: C.S. Lewis, J.R.R. Tolkien, Charles Williams, and Their Friends* (London, 1978).

Cavaliero, G. *Charles Williams: Poet of Theology* (London and Basingstoke, 1983).

Eliot, T.S. "The Significance of Charles Williams," *The Listener* 36.936 (December 19, 1946).

Hadfield, A.M. *An Introduction to Charles Williams* (London, 1959).

Horne, B. *Celebrating Charles Williams* (Leominster, 1995).

Lewis, C.S. "Preface," in ibid. (ed.), *Essays Presented to Charles Williams* (London, 1947).

Ridler, A. "Introduction," in Charles Williams, *The Image of the City and Other Essays* (London, 1958).

Shideler, M. McDermott. *The Theology of Romantic Love: A Study in the Writings of Charles Williams* (New York, 1962).

_____ *Charles Williams: A Critical Essay* (New York, 1966).

Urang, G. *Shadows of Heaven* (London, 1971).

Wylie, W.P. *The Pattern of Love* (London, 1958).

Chapter Seven (Leonid Ouspensky)

Writings

Essai sur la théologie de l'icône dans l'Eglise orthodoxe (Paris, 1960; E.t. Crestwood, N.Y., 1978).

Théologie de l'icône dans l'Eglise orthodoxe (Paris, 1980; E.t. Crestwood, N.Y., 1992).

"Symbolik des orthodoxen Kirchengebäudes und der Ikone," in E. Hammerschmidt (ed.), *Symbolik des orthodoxen und orientalischen Christentums*, 1 (= *Symbolik der Religionen*, Vol. 10, Stuttgart, 1962), pp. 53-90.

The Meaning of Icons (with V. Lossky) (Crestwood, N.Y., 1989, 3rd ed.).

Secondary Works

Bagley, J. *Icons and their Spiritual Significance* (London, 1987).

Doolan, S. *La redécouverte de l'Icône. La vie et l'oeuvre de Léonide Ouspensky* (Paris, 2001).

Nichols, R.L. "The Icon and the Machine in Russia's Religious Renaissance," in W.C. Brumfield and M.M. Velimirovic (eds.), *Christianity and the Arts in Russia* (Cambridge, 1991), pp. 131-144.

Onasch, K. and A.M. Schnieper. *Icons: The Fascination and the Reality* (New York, 1995).

Ouspensky, L. (Lydia). "Biographie de L.A. Ouspensky," in S. Doolan, *La redécouverte de l'Icône. La vie et l'oeuvre de Léonide Ouspensky* (Paris, 2001), pp. 9-12.

Scouteris, B. "A Great Iconographer and Theologian: Leonid Ouspensky (1902-1987)," in G. Limouris (ed.), *Icons: Windows on Eternity* (Geneva, 1990), pp. 213-216.

Chapter Eight (Jules Monchanin)

Writings

Benedictine Ashram (with H. Le Saux) (Douglas, 1964, 2nd ed.).

Entretiens 1955 (with J. Filliozat and A. Bareau) (Paris, 1956).

Esthétique et mystique, précédé de la Loi d'Exode, par Pierre Emmanuel (Paris, 1967).

Lettres à sa mère, 1913-1957 (Paris, 1989).

Lettres au père Le Saux, 1947-1957 (Paris, 1995).

Mystique de l'Inde, mystère chrétien: écrits et inédits. Présentés par S. Siauve (Paris, 1974).

In Quest of the Absolute, ed. J. Weber (Kalamazoo, Mich., and London, 1977), pp. 111-184.

Théologie et spiritualité missionaire (Paris, 1985).

Secondary Works

Abhishiktananda (H. Le Saux). *Hindu-Christian Meeting Point* (New Delhi, 1976, 2nd ed.).

Auctores varii. *Jules Monchanin, 1895-1957: regards croisés d'occident et d'orient. Actes des colloques de Lyon-Fleurie et de Shantivanam-Thannirpalli, avril-juin 1995* (Lyons, 1997).

Duperray, E. *L'abbé Jules Monchanin* (Bruges, 1956).

Jaquin, F. *Jules Monchanin, prêtre, 1895-1957* (Paris, 1996).

Lubac, H. de. *Images de l'abbé Monchanin* (Paris, 1967).

Mauro, G. *Ponte tra cultura european e cultura indiana. L'itinerario di Jules Monchanin, 1985-1957* (Rome, 2000).

Petit, J.G. *La jeunesse de Monchanin, 1895-1925: mystique et intelligence critique* (Paris, 1983).

Rodhe, S. *Jules Monchanin: Pioneer in Christian-Hindu Dialogue* (Delhi, 1993).

Stuart, J. *Swami Abhishiktananda: His Life Told Through His Letters* (New Delhi, 1995, 2nd ed.).

Weber, J. (ed.). *In Quest of the Absolute: The Life and Work of Jules Monchanin* (Kalamazoo, Mich., and London, 1977).